My life story as told to Warren Snaith Haviside

BUTCH

Butch
First published October 2011

© Butch James, Warren Snaith Haviside,
and Highbury Safika Media (Pty) Ltd
2004 03/1056/03, Highbury Safika Media, 21st floor, Metlife Centre,
7 Coen Steytler Avenue, Foreshore, 8001, Cape Town, South Africa

Managing Editor: Nick van Rensburg
Art Director: Wayne Jordaan
Proofreaders: Simon Borchardt, Philippa Byron, Dan Gillespie
Statistician: Eddie Grieb
Index: Linda Retief
Repro: Karin Livni, Donnevan van der Watt, Adri van der Watt,
Tammy-Anne Clarke, Naomi e'Camara, Claire Stockenström,
Craig McLeod
Cover Photo: Sean Laurentz
Other Photos: James collection, Gallo Images, Getty Images,
AFP Photo
Marketing Executive: Kim Schonfeldt
Printer: CTP Book Printers

CONTENTS

MESSAGE FROM WARREN SNAITH HAVISIDE

I'm sitting in Auckland during the 2011 Rugby World Cup and putting an author's note together almost feels as daunting as when I first started writing the opening paragraph to this book. Perhaps the best place to start would be at the beginning.

It was in 2008, I was working at an ad agency as a copywriter in London and recording an album at Abbey Road Studios with my band The Shotguns. Butch was based in Bath at the time and I frequently used to go and watch him play at The Recreation Ground. It was after one such game that I asked Butch if he had ever thought about putting a book together about his life story. I have known Butch since school and have followed his career closely. I thought it was phenomenal how he'd recovered from all his knee operations over the years and to go on to win a Rugby World Cup was mind blowing. He had been written off by many time and again and I thought the story of how he pulled himself out of those hard times would make for an inspiring read.

Once Butch had agreed, I would travel from London, tape recorder in hand, to Bath, where I'd spend a few hours at a time extracting the information I needed from him, and so the putting together of his life story was in motion. I started writing the book in London, took the first draft with me across to America, back to London, returned to South Africa and headed for the final stretch in New Zealand.

This book would not have been possible without the support and help of many people. Butch's family was extremely helpful in supplying me with information about Butch's childhood, so a big thanks to Mike, Jenny and Elton for being so forthcoming.

I had to contact many individuals, unions and clubs who had played a part in Butch's career. I would therefore like to thank Megan Harris and Mike Marnewick at the Sharks; Jimmy Wright, who was close to Butch throughout many of his recoveries, the staff at Dr Mark Ferguson's and Dr Willem van der Merwe's practices; Helen Bayes and Helen Shand at Bath RFC; rugby writer Mike Greenaway, for giving me a glimmer of hope; and Julia, Butch's wife, for providing me with valuable information and for reading my first drafts as a bedtime story to him!

Butch has taught me a lot during the writing of this book and I've managed to experience and dwell on the real Butch James more than most get to do. Butch is extremely humble and has a huge amount of drive and determination despite his carefree demeanour. His never-say-die attitude is something we can all admire him for. The fact that he made the Springbok squad for the 2011 Rugby World Cup, after being told several years ago that he might never play again, is awe-inspiring. It's also been admirable to see how he's matured and how he accepted his role as a senior at the 2011 World Cup – he put the team's goals and needs above his own. Butch has been my rugby hero for the past 10 years and that makes the writing of this book extremely special to me.

Thanks must also go out to everyone at Highbury Safika Media. I know this book would have been little more than a folder on my laptop if it wasn't for you. I must single out a few people here: Mark Keohane for opening the door, Tony Walker for making things happen, Simon Borchardt for getting the ball rolling, Kim Schonfeldt and Tamlyn Pasqualie for the marketing and PR, and Wayne Jordaan for the art direction. Last but not least, Nick van Rensburg, who as managing editor kept the ship stable and on course when the pressure was really on.

Thanks also to Eddie Grieb for compiling Butch's stats and to Linda Retief for the index.

I hope that I have done Butch's story justice and trust you will enjoy the insight into Butch's life.

In closing I'd like to thank my family – Mom, Dad and Candice, my close friends and all the guys at Sugar. Thank you for all your unwavering support throughout the writing of this book. You have all been extremely understanding and supportive.

I dedicate the writing of this book to my son, Tristan.

MESSAGE FROM JOHN SMIT

Being asked by Butchie to write a foreword for his book is such a privilege for me. I've known Butchie since 1998, when we first shared a digs together with some other interesting chaps, so I'm sure this book is going to be like reading a highlights package of my time spent with him!

Butchie is the easiest guy in the world to get along with and definitely one of the greatest characters the game in South Africa has had. His team-mates love him, enjoy having him around and really, really love how he smashes in to anyone who dares come into the vacuum! He is always a treat on tour and has an ability to get guys through a five-week trip with ease.

His best trait is not his tackling, or his silky smooth skills or his no-look pass, but his heart, which is why rugby will not be the only thing that defines this man. His family and friends love him and he loves them; he is happiest when surrounded by his mates and family.

I have been lucky enough to grow up with him and see him struggle through numerous knee operations, play nearly 50 Test matches, win a World Cup, get married and mature through the years. At stages during our younger days I felt more like a big brother than a mate to him, but I'm delighted to call him my friend and couldn't be prouder of him and what he has achieved.

1

A BOY CALLED BUTCH

The words 'Go Springboks' had been written across the windows of the office block opposite our team hotel in Paris, the Sofitel Bercy, quite near the city centre. Staff from the company over the road were obviously chuffed by our presence and keen for us to pump England in the final.

It was good to know the French were pulling for us but the week leading up to the World Cup final was nevertheless extremely tense because it was ours to lose and England's to win. My family and close friends had arrived in Paris during the week and I could feel by their presence that we had the entire country back home behind us.

It was here. The time had arrived. We were in the 2007 Rugby World Cup final and we had to deliver, that was non-negotiable. This was the crowning moment of the special partnership which had been built between this group of players and our coach, Jake White – a partnership which had started years ago when the core of this World Cup team had won the Sanzar/UAR U21 Championship (which would later become the World Cup for this age group) in Buenos Aires in 1999.

When Jake took over as Bok coach in 2004, he told the team that he had a plan, which culminated in the Springboks winning the 2007 World Cup in France.

I wasn't part of the team during this period as I was recovering from a series of crippling knee injuries, but it was a plan from which Jake never wavered. The Boks suffered a setback when they lost 20-26 to France at the Stade de France in 2005 but the guys told me how Jake had them refocus on the ultimate goal as they huddled in the dressing room, trying to come to terms with what had been a poor performance. Instead of getting down on the guys Jake said something along the lines of: 'In two years' time we're going to be back in this dressing room and the only thing that's going to be different is that there's going to be a gold trophy in the middle of the circle.'

And now we had reached the final pit stop along that journey. The Springboks were in the World Cup final. My bag was packed and I was ready. I made my way down to the lobby of the hotel where the team was meeting. There was a silent, steely resolve about the boys. It didn't get any bigger than this. Nerves were flying big time!

Our team bus arrived and we headed for St-Denis, towards the Stade de France and our date with destiny – the 2007 Rugby World Cup final, rugby's biggest showdown. Our wives, girlfriends and some close friends and family were on another bus behind us as we steadily made our way through the Paris traffic towards the stadium. We were being escorted by French police and the sirens and hooting of the cars as we passed made it seem even more chaotic than it already was.

There was pure silence on the bus. You could feel the tension and mental energy. All the injuries, the operations, the broken bones, the years spent on crutches, the ridiculous allegations of using anabolic steroids and dealing in cocaine, all the bans I'd received for dangerous tackles, all the flak I had taken from the people back home who didn't believe in me, it just fell away. None of it mattered anymore. All the ups and downs of this career of mine had led to this – the biggest game of my life.

I didn't care about anything else but winning this game. I had been through so much in the past eight or so years of my professional career but none of it seemed to matter compared to what was now at stake. I also thought about how the Sharks had managed to stuff up in the Super 14 final five months earlier, fighting back gnawing thoughts that it was going to happen again.

It's difficult to explain what you think of at a time like that, what emotions you're going through. I suppose you run through how you want to play the game, and what your role is going to be. It was all a bit of a blur really, even though it was all familiar territory for us, having played England in our pool game and Argentina in our semi-final at the magnificent stadium, which had been built for the Fifa World Cup in 1998.

We arrived at the Stade de France, got changed and went through our warm-up drills out on the field; aware of the stadium filling up, of the noise, the occasional shout from a fan but also trying to block it out. Jake was trying to keep us all as calm as possible but I could see he was tense. We went back to the change room, where John Smit reminded us of everything we'd been through together, emphasising how long we'd planned and worked towards the 80 minutes that lay before us.

The sound of 'London Calling' by The Clash was ringing out over the stadium PA and you could hear all the English supporters getting revved up. There were hordes of them there that night and we were certainly outnumbered in terms of support. But we knew we had a whole nation glued to their TV sets and we knew we had to come through for everyone back home.

If you could take all the tension felt in every single living room, every club and every pub in South Africa and add it to the tension inside the Stade de France that night, that's what we were feeling. It's the kind of stress that can make a grown man puke.

Then the call came. We left the change room; down the dank corridors and on to the field to line up for the spine-chilling ritual of singing the national anthems. 'God Save the Queen' was obviously a shitload louder than 'Nkosi Sikelel' iAfrika' but we weren't fazed. You only need to look for your family's faces in the crowd to stay in control of the adrenaline pumping through your veins and the emotion welling up in your eyes. This was everything I had dreamed of from a young age, and was a moment I had worked tirelessly towards throughout my extraordinary and challenging career.

My knees have gone through five ACL (anterior cruciate ligament) reconstructions and three cartilage operations. I've had six broken bones in my body. I've had a thousand massive collisions in my career and I've been under the surgeon's knife 11 times. I've also managed to become the most capped Springbok flyhalf in history.

Without further ado, let me tell you about the fun and frustration, the school of hard knocks and what it's like being Butch.

I was born at the new Johannesburg General Hospital on 8 January 1979 at 12:45pm and weighed in at 3.1kg. I was the second son to Mike and Jenny James and was named Andrew David James after two of my dad's good friends who had recently passed away, one in a diving accident and the other in an airplane crash.

It had been a long wait for my mom. She had been hospitalised with toxemia for eight weeks prior to my birth.

It was a trying time for the family. We had just relocated to Johannesburg. Elton, my older brother by two-and-a-half years, was sent back to Durban to live with our grandmother and grandfather, as my dad was still juggling work and his professional football career.

My dad was known in football circles as 'The Horse'. His nickname was due to his running ability and fierce defence. He would apparently be given instructions to keep a certain member of the opposing team out of the game, and he did just that; with a lethal efficiency that, I'm told, was almost too cruel to watch.

Dad was always modest about his football exploits, but I've heard from some of his team-mates and others who watched him that he was an exceptionally good footballer.

His favourite position was at centre forward. In the old days before unity was achieved in South African sport he captained the SA Whites in the memorable first multiracial football tournament to be held in South Africa. The team line-up included the SA Coloureds, SA Blacks, SA Indians and SA Continentals – who eventually ended up beating my dad's team in the final.

Dad also played alongside the great Archie Soekoe in the South African side that beat Malcolm Allison's British All Stars 2-1 in a thrilling, action-packed game at the Rand Stadium. Unfortunately, he had to relinquish the honour of captaining the South African XI that competed against the 1976 touring Argentinean side due to cartilage problems (like father, like son) and was forced to watch the match from the sidelines.

Never one to be held down by setbacks, Dad transferred to Durban United in 1977 and in that same year he earned his official Springbok colours.

In one game they thrashed neighbours Rhodesia (now Zimbabwe) 7-0 at the Rand Stadium. However, in the return match in Rhodesia the teams drew 1-1; thanks to the heroics of the Rhodesian goalkeeper who held the South Africans at bay – a bloke by the name of Bruce Grobbelaar, who later starred for Liverpool.

In 1978, when the NFL (National Football League) club Durban United was sold to Verulam Suburbs, who were in the Federation League, my dad became involved in a controversial argument with the Federation hierarchy. The upshot of that was that he was denied the opportunity of representing his country because of petty political squabbles between the Federation and NPSL (National Professional Soccer League) leagues. He was subsequently banned for life from the Federation. Politics and sport. Need I say more?

My dad's next move was to NPSL side Wits University, where he captained the team and was named Footballer of the Year at the club's awards ceremony. However, tragedy struck in 1980 when Dad broke his right leg in a match against Pilkington United. The break took two years to heal and my dad was forced to announce his retirement from the game on this very sad note.

Towards the end of 1980 we relocated to Cape Town and were reunited as a family. It was a happy time for all of us and my folks have often told me how Elton loved having his baby brother around. According to Mom and Dad I was a happy and robust baby. I walked early and showed signs of enjoying balls of all shapes and sizes. If there was a ball lying around I wanted to get my hands on the thing.

It was an exciting new chapter in my early life and we had bought our first house – I should say Mom and Dad bought a house – in Somerset West near Cape Town. It was three months before we could move into our new home, so for the first month we stayed in a hotel in Strand – which is literally just across the road from the beach, hence the name. (Strand means 'beach' in Afrikaans.)

Elton loved to swim but I hated the water. I really couldn't stand it. So Mom would have to sit halfway up the beach watching Elton in the sea while keeping one eye on me, haring up and down the promenade on my yellow plastic BP scooter.

These were exhausting times for my mom. The days were long as in summer the sun in Cape Town doesn't go down until about 8pm. The hotel was fine in terms of holidays – but not for two little livewires like Elton and myself.

My grandfather passed away on 6 January 1981 in Durban. We flew up as a family to be with my grandmother and this was when she gave me the nickname Butch. She said I looked angelic but seemed extraordinarily tough and strong for my age. My grandmother used to recall how I'd fall down the back staircase and then get up and run to the swing in the garden and off I'd go – swinging away as if absolutely nothing had happened.

My gran couldn't believe how well I could hit a ball, kick a ball, catch a ball and throw a ball for a two-year-old – and so she decided Butch suited my actions and mannerisms better than Andrew. I think I preferred it too, and that's what I've been called ever since – Butch.

When we returned to the Cape, Elton and I had the joy of living in a caravan park for two months before we moved into our house. This was a much better environment than a hotel for two boys. The caravan was awesome to stay in as a kid and there were other youngsters around for us to play with too. It was obviously not as glamorous for my dad, who would leave the caravan in a suit every day and go to work. My working-class hero!

My early days of childhood were by all accounts modest and my parents did the best they could to get me my sports equipment. It didn't help that I had expensive tastes and, as many youngsters do, I always wanted the big-name brands; you know, the stuff my idols wore or used.

Presents on my birthday and at Christmas would almost always consist of some or other piece of sports equipment.

Mom and Dad spent any spare money they had on getting me my sports gear and things were often tight at the end of the month because of that. You find that kind of sacrifice and backing in the backgrounds of many top-class sportsmen and I will always be extremely grateful for the role my parents played in my career.

When it came to discussing new equipment like cricket bats or boots, my dad would always say things like: 'In my day we used to put cardboard under the soles of our shoes and put drawing pins in to turn normal shoes into athletics spikes … in my day we would sand down our cricket bats at the end of every season, oil them, and put them away in the cupboard so that they were ready for the next season.' Without fail, any conversation we would have about sports equipment would start with 'in my day', and the phrase has become quite the household joke as the years have passed.

March arrived and we moved into our new home – our first together as a family. The house was in Land en Zeezicht (Land and Seaview) in Somerset West and the suburb was a very special place. We had everything on our doorstep: a BMX track and shops at the end of the road where Elton and I could spend our R2 pocket money on sweets; a nature reserve; Radloff Park Sports Complex a block away and Beaumont Primary School two blocks away.

The Heidelberg mountain range framed this whole area on the one side with the sweep of False Bay on the other. There can't be a more perfect setting for two youngsters to explore and get up to a bit of mischief, so Eltie and I did just that.

The day we moved into our first home, Sue and Barry Barnett, along with their sons Wayne and David (whom we'd met while living at the caravan park), offered to look after Elton and myself for the day while the folks moved. During the course of the day I went missing and the Barnett family went absolutely ballistic. They were frantic and got themselves into a right old panic. They spent hours looking for me and at one stage were absolutely convinced that I had been kidnapped.

They looked all over – but still no sign of Butch. First they searched the swimming pool, then the ablution facilities and then the area outside the caravan park premises; they combed over the suburb. As you can imagine, they were in an absolute state. What on earth were they going to tell my folks? 'Umm … sorry, but we lost your son.'

The search party continued throughout the afternoon and into the evening until I was finally found – fast asleep on the metal stairs leading to our old caravan. I must have wandered off while they were looking for me and then returned to the caravan without being spotted. Needless to say I didn't understand what the fuss was about when they woke me up. They were all standing there with shattered nerves, while I was recovering from a *lekker* kip.

I got my first BMX in 1982. I loved that bike. I would meet my mates every afternoon and we would play at the BMX track until dark. That year I also attended swimming lessons with a lady by the name of Cathy Moses. My folks wanted to get a small pool built at home and felt it necessary that I learned to swim. However, the pool was put in before the lessons started, in the days before pool nets. One day Elton heard a splash in the back garden. He immediately ran to the pool and found me with my head barely above water and frantically trying to keep afloat.

Elton hauled me out of the pool in the nick of time; a few seconds later and who knows how this escapade might have ended? It was because of this incident that I hated going under water. I even used to put up a huge performance when my mom had to wash my hair in the bath. But I am proud to say that this specific summer I became water safe, thanks to Cathy. If it wasn't for her I would have probably never have got to enjoy my surfing as much as I do today.

In 1984 I started at Happy Days pre-school and unlike most kids my age I couldn't wait to go. I loved the interaction and the entertainment. They had an old car to play in as well as a track to ride scooters on, with road signs and all. Elton and I also started playing at the local soccer club. At this stage of our lives soccer was our biggest passion. We couldn't get enough and would practise and play whenever we could without caring about the cold and rainy Cape winters. Our matches would be on Saturday mornings and in the afternoons my dad, who had been talked out of retirement, would play, but Elton and I hardly watched as we were engrossed in our two-against-two contests on the sidelines.

I took to football immediately and the talented genes passed on by my dad were there for all to see. I was known by my opponents as 'the blond boy' and parents from the opposing side would often shout from the sideline, 'Watch out for the blond boy!' They might have added an additional descriptive name or two!

I really loved it and thrived on being out on the pitch. For most of my young days I dreamed about being a pro soccer player one day, just like my dad.

My dad spent a lot of time with us, teaching us skills and passing on his sporting knowledge. But he never put any pressure on us to play. He'd only take us kicking and stuff if we asked him to. He never forced us or pushed us. I was also lucky to have an older brother to play against. Elton and I would take that practice and turn it into play and I know that those days had an influence on what I achieved in sport. I learned a lot from playing all kinds of games against him. It was tough playing against an older, bigger opponent but that's where I developed my instinct to take it head on. There's nothing like match practice and, believe you me, I got a lot of that growing up. Elton was very competitive, really good at a variety of sports and there were many disputes involving the James boys on the front lawn.

Our little Test matches often resulted in a bit of rough play – but hey, who says you can't bend the rules when there's no referee watching over the game?

Elton provided me with a huge amount of inspiration years later when I watched him play at Kings Park in Durban for the Natal U21 rugby side. It was then that I realised I wanted to follow in his footsteps and play rugby at Kings Park one day.

Elton's a great brother and I owe a lot of my success to him. He tries his hardest never to miss any of my games. He flew back to South Africa from England for my Springbok debut and always sends me inspiring messages and letters. He's a real beaut, and an awesome older brother. It was great to thank Elton for the role he had played in my life when, during the build-up to the Rugby World Cup in 2007, we were allowed to invite a person who had inspired us to a team-building exercise on the South Coast. Each invitee was presented with a 2007 World Cup jersey inscribed with the message: 'Thanks for making a difference in my life – RWC 2007.' I also wrote a personal message in Eltie's jersey.

I spent my formative school years at Beaumont Primary. I was there from Grade 1 to Grade 5 – although in my day we used to call it Class 1 to Standard 3.

In those five years I swam, played cricket, rugby and did athletics for my school. I represented Western Province in soccer and baseball and represented Boland in athletics.

In my first few days of rugby at Beaumont I tackled the daylights out of my own team-mate, who had the ball and was running the wrong way. The coach wasn't impressed.

I thought it was a really good tackle, though, and was rather chuffed with myself. Out of such small incidents do big habits grow?

We had neighbours who owned a horse and riding it became a fascination of mine. I used to eye the horse out and was really keen to give it a go, so one day I lied to them by telling them I knew how to ride. My persuasiveness worked and they allowed me to go for a little trot. I jumped on and the horse immediately took off at a gallop. It hadn't run for more than 50m when it threw me. I hit the ground with real force. Anyone who knows what it's like coming off a horse at pace will tell you that it's not a joke. Well, that was me – winded with the skin off my knees and the horse setting out for the great wide open.

My parents helped us for the rest of the afternoon as we tried to rescue the horse from disappearing into the streets of Somerset West. Needless to say, I don't think I've ever ridden a horse since. I'll leave that kind of stuff to Butch Cassidy.

Once, my mom and dad attended a wedding in the area close to our house. They left Elton and me at home and gave us some pocket money to spend at the nearby shops. First it was off to pedal wildly around Radloff Park, where I took my eye off the ball, and took a tumble down a bank into a dry river bed.

My mom and dad had to leave the wedding and come to the rescue. They took me to the doctor, who told me my arm was broken and put it in plaster of paris. The following day my mom asked us to take her to where I had fallen. She was absolutely mortified to see that I had fallen down a height of about 3m into a dry, rocky donga. The worst part of it was that my bike landed on top of me – as if the fall wasn't enough!

What had happened was that I was riding alongside the river bank and there were reeds covering the ground. I never saw the drop and literally rode over the edge.

Fortunately, there were people having a picnic close by and they came to my rescue. Elton pushed both our bikes home, as I was in too much pain, but it took me about two hours to convince him there was something seriously wrong. Two hours with a broken arm? Not fun! The funny thing is that my parents had said to us before walking out of the front door, 'Don't phone us unless there is a real problem'. That was not the first or last time I would be seeing the doctor for a fractured limb.

Our eight or so years spent in Cape Town were great. We got to see a lot of the Cape, met fantastic people and made lifelong friends.

Our next move came in the late-80s when I was 10 years old, and it proved to be a significant moment in my life – to Pietermaritzburg in the KwaZulu-Natal Midlands. I was enrolled at Merchiston Preparatory School, an obvious move as Dad was an old 'Merchie Mud Rat' – the name given to Merchiston pupils because of the school's location on the banks of the Msunduzi River, the water course on which KZN's famous Duzi Canoe Marathon is staged every year.

The river is notorious for flooding and when it used to break its banks you'd see all the boys 'duck diving' and playing rugby in the rain. Duck diving is basically running as fast as you can towards a huge puddle of water that has gathered on the sports field, then diving and skidding for metres on your belly and chest when you hit the water. All for the love of water and mud! A few hours of this and the boys did indeed start to resemble soaked rats, so the name Merchie Mud Rats was pretty apt.

Merchiston is well-known in the area and, as it's the main feeder school to Maritzburg College, set me on the path that one day would culminate with me earning Springbok rugby colours. South African cricketing legends such as Jackie McGlew and Jonty Rhodes also had the distinction of being Mud Rats. I was fortunate that my cousin, Darren, was in the same standard as me so slotting in wasn't a problem.

I had an excellent three years there. I tried every sport that was made available to us – squash, hockey, swimming and tennis, over and above playing my regular sports which were cricket, rugby and soccer. That's when I was happiest – outdoors, playing sport.

It was at Merchiston that I met Peter Cameron, Craig Harris and Ross Wilson. We would remain the best of mates throughout our school days and are good buddies to this day. To put it bluntly – I think we were any teacher's worst nightmare. I was well-acquainted with the phrase 'six of the best' and many a time, blame for the punishment could be traced back to the actions of my mates.

One day Pete and I were sitting next to each other in class and for no rhyme or reason Pete suddenly hit his desk as hard as he could with his ruler. It made such a loud cracking sound as it broke that I lifted off my chair. Before I knew what was going on, Pete told the teacher that I had just hit him with the ruler; he was playing the victim.

I tried to defend myself and ended up winding up the teacher in the process, who thought I was lying, while Pete insisted it was me who had hit him. The upshot was that we both ended up feeling the business end of a cane for 'disruptive behaviour' – a term that would turn up again later in my rugby career!

In Standard 5 (Grade 7) Craig, Pete and I were cast in a Zulu play. Craig came from a farming background and could speak fluent Zulu. So every time he started speaking, he sounded like a proper Zulu. When it came to the live performance we couldn't contain ourselves and when Craig delivered his lines, Pete and I would just burst out laughing. We absolutely ruined the play!

We couldn't stop laughing but we did push our luck too far, and the teacher eventually made us cane each other as punishment. The master gave Pete the cane and told him to lay into me. He hit me quite hard actually – perhaps a little softer than the teacher might have – and much to the absolute pleasure of Mr Peter Cameron I might add.

Next it was Craig's turn to dish out the punishment with Pete on the receiving end. But being a good oke and a mate, Craig gave Pete a soft tap. The teacher absolutely lost it and told us that if we didn't do a proper job he would get hold of all three of us. So I had no choice and did what any noble friend would do to save the team – I laid into Craig. We left the room and Craig started crying because his backside was on fire, wailing actually – it was one of the funniest things ever! I mean, what would you have done? What are friends for? And after all that we still got 'jacks' from the teacher anyway as he said we hadn't done a good enough job.

I spent many school holidays with the Harris family. They farmed in the Greytown area, about an hour out of Pietermaritzburg. I used to enjoy going out there with them.

We used to ride motorbikes all over the farm and go fishing and hunting. After one trip I went home to my folks with a duiker, a small antelope common to KZN, which I had shot. Dad was really proud of my first buck and set about getting out the tools and condiments needed to make biltong – only for me to dowse his enthusiasm by pointing out that I had shot the poor buck three times with a shotgun to make sure it was dead. The meat was riddled with pellets and my old man was not impressed at all.

I was young and scared of animals, as most are at that age. I wouldn't do that sort of thing now.

The next occasion I went hunting it was a father-and-son outing. I must add that we enjoyed these types of activities together but by no means were we big-game hunters of the wild outdoors.

We were dropped off at a certain spot on the farm and were told to take cover and camouflage ourselves. So we found a quiet spot under a tree. We nestled in there and hid, waiting patiently for something to appear. We waited and waited. But as time passed we began chatting.

The conversation between my dad and I sounded a little like this:

Dad: 'Hey Butch, what do you think this knife is for?'

Me: 'I don't know, what do you think?'

Dad: 'I think if you shoot a buck you have to slit its throat with this …'

Me: 'I am definitely not going to slit the buck's throat!'

Just then a huge trophy bushbuck came running along. It stopped and stood about 25m from us. We were amazed at our luck and immediately took aim. The buck was in both our sights.

Dad: 'You shoot, Butch.'

Me: 'No Dad, you shoot it.'

Dad: 'No, you take it.'

Me: 'No, really, it's yours.'

This went on until the buck took off and disappeared without a single bullet being fired. Dad and I were obviously embarrassed but what can you do? We looked at each other and just burst out laughing.

There is an Afrikaans term for this behaviour called 'bok-koors', which means 'buck fever'. It's when the hunter gets so overwhelmed by the presence of the buck that he can't get himself to pull the trigger. I am told it even happens to the great hunters of this world.

I don't know if it was actually *bok-koors* or whether both of us were just too chicken to slit the buck's throat but father and son returned to the camp with all bullets intact and no buck to brag about.

They were idyllic days, the ones I spent at Merchiston. My big sporting highlight was making the Natal junior Craven Week side at flyhalf in Standard 5, my final year in primary school. I suppose you can say that's when the die was cast. I had been bitten by the bug and rugby was going to be my game.

2

THE RED, BLACK, AND WHITE

My high school years were happily spent at Maritzburg College, one of the country's greatest educational institutions and the fertile nursery for many a fine KwaZulu-Natal sportsman. 'College', as the school is known, had a huge impact on my life and career. This great school was founded in 1863 and was built to accommodate the children of an influx of settlers arriving in the new city of Pietermaritzburg and its surrounding farmlands.

As the school grew, architects were commissioned to build a larger classroom and boarding block. This was completed in 1888 and later became known as Clark House, honouring the school's third headmaster – Mr RD Clark. Clark House is a magnificent landmark that carries South Africa's heritage seal, certifying it as a national monument.

The Victoria Hall, which is joined on to Clark House and served as a British Army hospital during the Second Boer

War, was also declared a national monument, making it a hallowed and special place. You can feel something in your bones when you walk around Clark House and Victoria Hall. History and tradition seeps out of the walls.

There's a legend that's passed down among the boarders of the school that anyone who attempts to go into the Victoria Hall at midnight and touch the brass plaque when the full moon is out will break a limb while attempting it. I think it's just because it's so bloody scary in there at night – boys have probably broken their legs and arms by trying to get the hell out of there as fast as possible, but it's not the cause of one of the many broken bones I have had to endure!

You could go to the College sports grounds on any given afternoon in those days and you'd find boys playing touch rugby or 'domp' – a game that developed among College boys on rainy days when organised sport was called off.

Domp is basically a rugby game with no set phases, so the ball just keeps doing the rounds, and I'm sure it's the root cause for College boys learning to tackle with such vigour and fire.

College rugby is notorious for its fierce defence and it's because of domp. It was a great way to get your own back on a senior who had been giving you a hard time. You quickly got rid of your fear of size by playing domp. It didn't matter if you were the smallest junior or the biggest senior in the 1st XV, you all played against each other in two teams of about 50 boys a side and you had to get stuck in.

There were always a few concussions, some broken bones, bloody noses, you name it. But at the end of the day it's what bonded the boys together – a sort of fight club if you like. What happened down on those fields stayed there. No whingeing. You just got on with it, which I have to say is a great way to look at life as a whole.

There was a little chap who was a year or two below me by the name of Gregg Fry – many know him today as 'Piggy'.

He had to say please to me, as he was a junior (juniors had to say the word 'please' at the end of every sentence when addressing a senior, unless the senior told you not to, which meant you were mates). In the midst of a helter-skelter game of domp, the ball came out to Piggy. I lined him up and hit him full taps but it was about a minute late! He hit the ground and was so badly winded that he lost all thoughts of respect and let out a moan, 'Fuck you, Butch'. That's the day we became mates. Piggy never had to say please to me again and it turned out to be a very good friendship to make. Today Piggy is my brother-in-law and we're the best of friends.

Piggy has tackled me on a few boys' nights out but reckons it would take another 15 hits for him to get even.

College's rigorous structures and traditions date back to pre-1900 British boarding schools and is perhaps the only school in the country where these norms are retained to their original extent.

Your first year at College is like being in the army. You are drilled – but it's all for the good. You can go to College at lunchtime and watch how the first years line up for food and have to sprint across the quad between the Victoria Hall and Clark House. It's a place that instils respect.

First years have to sprint on the quad, may not talk, have to stand to attention at all times, may not walk on grass, have to sprint in front of Clark House, cannot walk on cobbled stone, or higher ground, may not have a middle parting in their hair, must greet every senior that passes by his surname – and there's no excuse for not knowing a name!

You may not put your hands in your pockets and you have to sprint when setting foot on the sacred ground of Goldstones – the famous rugby field where all 1st XV games are staged.

Over the years, many Old Collegians and parents have questioned College's customs but to me it is what makes the boys who come out of this school and is exactly what underpins the school's ethos.

College's crest is a red shield with a crossed carbine and assegai (a short Zulu spear) over a Latin scroll, *Proaris Et Focus*, which means 'For Hearth and Home'.

The colours of red, black and white are a reference to the wars fought between the British and the Zulus – the black and white representing the warring parties, and the red representing the blood that was spilt between them.

It was a special privilege and my rare good fortune to have been able to attend Maritzburg College. Notable former Old Collegians include Henry Nourse, founder of Nourse Mines and former chairman of the South African Olympic Committee; Judge Walter Thrash, a former South African senator and a former judge president of Natal; Alan Paton, author of *Cry, The Beloved Country*; HG 'Nummy' Deane and Jackie McGlew, former captains of the South African cricket team; Cuan McCarthy, former SA fast bowler; Philip Nel, captain of the great Springbok rugby side that defeated the All Blacks in New Zealand in 1937; Hubert Freakes, former England rugby union player; Keith Oxlee, one of the great Springbok flyhalves; and Andy van der Watt, a champion sprinter and Springbok wing.

The list goes on and on: Cedric Savage, former CEO and chairman of the Tongaat Hulett group and former captain of the SA waterpolo team; Paul Harris, CEO of First Rand Group; Joel Stransky, the Springbok flyhalf who kicked the drop goal that won the 1995 Rugby World Cup (more on Joel later); Jonty Rhodes, legendary South African cricketer and one of the greatest fielders the game has seen.

I'm sure I have left out many other distinguished College old boys and for that I sincerely apologise. In a nutshell, College is the oldest boys' high school in KwaZulu-Natal; it has produced more than 180 international sportsmen, 23 South African captains and a number of Olympians.

One of its most colourful former scholars was Bill Payn, who played provincial sport in five disciplines, represented the Springboks against the British Isles side of 1924, and gained everlasting fame by running the 1922 Comrades Marathon (a gruelling 90km) in his rugby boots, as if running the Comrades in a pair of Nikes isn't crazy enough.

In my first year at College I played for the U13A rugby side and a game against Glenwood in Durban provided me with an amazing moment for the memory bank – for different reasons. I broke my arm really badly and ended up being taken off on a stretcher, where none other than a man by the name of Joel Stransky helped carry me off the field and into the ambulance.

Joel was a friend of our coach, Mr Lance Veenstra, and was there to watch the game. Pretty freaky that both of us went to College, both of us would become Springboks and both of us would get a Rugby World Cup winner's medal. We're all sewn into the fabric of the universe in some or other way.

I was taken to St Augustine's Hospital, moaning all the way. My arm was so badly broken that it had an S-bend in it. I was in a lot of pain. The doctor took one look at me and hauled me into the theatre to manipulate the arm back and put it in plaster. My mom came to visit me in the afternoon and my enthusiasm for rugby was undimmed – we watched the Sharks on TV from my hospital bed.

My mom stayed with me that night as my dad was away on a golfing trip. He picked us up on Sunday morning and we immediately sought a second opinion from our orthopaedic surgeon in Pietermaritzburg. He said the break was a bad one and decided that an immediate operation was necessary to insert steel pins and a plate.

The staff who had worked on me at St Augustine's had to cut my rugby jersey off me and my mom had to sew it back together again because we didn't have money to waste on a new one.

In the meantime Elton had been sent to Alexandra High School. This was very difficult for me, as there was always an intense rivalry between the schools – mainly due to its location. Alex was virtually across the road from College.

Elton later moved across to College – but the years he spent at Alex were awful for me on match days. This is because, as I said, Elton was good … really good. When the 1st XVs played I would be in the predicament of hoping he would do something brilliant, but I still had College's interests at heart. It was really tough. When he had to kick for poles my entire school was hoping he would miss, while secretly I'd be hoping like hell that he was successful. Yep – blood is indeed a lot thicker than water. Elton was head boy in his final year at Alex and always displayed great leadership skills – that's why he was a great role model for me.

But I am pleased to say that it was really cool when Elton came across to College for his final year as a post-matric. He was a good fullback and it was great seeing him in the red, black and white.

The next year at rugby trials my bottom lip was split so badly that I had to get it repaired by a plastic surgeon – you can still see the lump. I had a hectic year but luckily, besides this incident, it was accident-free. My coach that year was the late Mr LP Zaayman. He once went up to my dad at the Collegians Club and said, 'That son of yours has a real rugby brain on him – he's going to go far.' LP – also known by College boys as Zappy – predicted a bright future for me and I wish he had been around to witness the 2007 Rugby World Cup.

The year 1994 was probably the only incident-free one I had in sport. And I mean ever.

I told my mom one school holiday in '94 that I was going to the Kokstad tennis tournament. This was a big thing for all the kids who went to Hilton College, Michaelhouse, Maritzburg College, Maritzburg Girls' High, St John's Girls'

School, St Anne's and Wykeham Collegiate. All the schools in the area highlighted this date in the calendar – it was the one social event that no boy or girl in their teens wanted to miss. Thank goodness for that. I mean, what would a tennis tournament be without a mixed doubles partner?

On the day I was being picked up to go to the tournament, my mom asked me what racket I was going to take and was shocked by my reply: 'We're not playing, *Ma*, we're the supporters' club.' All the boys met at my place, and in one of my friend's tog bags was a whole lot of, well, liquid refreshment. As we walked to the car all you could hear was the noise of bottles clinking together. My mom didn't pick up on it, though – I think it never crossed her mind that we would get up to antics like drinking at that age.

If there was naughtiness in the air I would never be far away. I remember getting the cane a few times because I used to speak Afrikaans in an American accent in Miss Strydom's class. It used to drive her up the wall, but it did sound funny and my mates loved it. I used to profess that that was just the way I spoke Afrikaans. Needless to say she never fell for it and I would end up with three of the best. And let me tell you, at Maritzburg College, just like most of the other great boys' schools in South Africa, that meant a bloody good hiding because some of the masters there had swings that Ernie Els would be proud of.

My Standard 9 (Grade 11) year was a gruelling one on the sports field and the one in which the knee problems that would dog me for the rest of my career started. While playing for the U16A side against Kearsney, I went down in a tackle, felt a stab of pain in my knee and heard a huge snapping sound. I tried to carry on – being the relentless fool that I can be sometimes – but I had to leave the field in pain and head for the first of many knee operations.

A scope was done on the knee and the decision was taken not to operate until my bones had fully developed. The operation was done in the middle of the following year, when I was in matric, which meant no rugby.

Luckily I have always been a very obedient patient, taken my injuries seriously and done everything I was told to by the book. I went to physio and to gym to work on a special set of instructions. The rehabilitation took some time, but as soon as I was ready I was back out on the sports field.

It wasn't long, though, before I was back in surgery for a second time to get the knee sorted out. By this stage soccer had disappeared from my life and I must say it did sadden me at times. I was young and still didn't know what the future held, but what I did know was that I missed soccer big time.

I was nearing my final years at school and all I wanted was my learner's driver's licence. I got the vital slip of paper the day after I turned 17. No wasting time in that department.

Other developments were also entering our lives. I was invited to a Girls' High School dance and told my mom we needed to get a dozen roses. I forced her to take me into town in search of these 12 vital items. I was quite adamant about the exact number and my mom became irritable but curious at the same time. Eventually she couldn't contain herself and enquired who the special lady was. She was most unimpressed when I replied that they were actually for each of my mates who were boarders and couldn't get out to buy their own roses.

In my matric year, with rugby out of the question because of my knee injury, I played 2nd XI cricket. I really enjoyed my cricket and was what you'd call an all-rounder's all-rounder. And that doesn't mean batting and bowling.

I was an all-rounder in the extreme sense of the word, squeezing every last bit of juice out of the game. I used to keep wicket for 25 overs, then take off the pads and bowl somewhere in the next 25 before wielding a mean willow when it was our turn to bat.

At one stage I thought cricket was going to be my main sport and that I might go further in cricket than in rugby, especially seeing as my early rugby career had already been hampered by knee injuries. One of my cricket team-mates at College was none other than Kevin Pietersen. KP was a special kind of individual. We got to know each other well and even then you could see that he possessed a huge amount of self-belief. Whether he was playing in the A or B team, Kevin always believed he was the best man for the job. He's always been the same guy he is today. Call it what you will, some say he's arrogant or a braggart, but perhaps it's just called backing yourself against all odds. He's done really well, so hats off to him.

Just like mine, KP's career has not always been plain sailing. He too was ridiculed and written off by a large portion of the public, but he's managed to bounce back a stronger and better player when it's mattered.

Match days on Saturday at College were always special occasions with an atmosphere around Goldstones that had to be experienced to be believed. College old boys and staff had an agreement that the main field would never be watered so it resembled a big slab of tarmac. Not without reason, Goldstones is notorious for being the hardest schoolboy field in South Africa.

To put it quite bluntly, the private schoolboys used to shit themselves having to take us on, on Goldstones. It was said that when a visiting side ran on to the field at College, the scoreboard would have them 10-0 down purely because Goldstones was harder than cement during rugby season.

I can remember the afternoon sun slanting through the big trees, casting beams of light across the field and on to Basher Ridge. The ringing of ice cream bells and that haunting chant of 'Red, Black, White' echoing across the grounds when we used to leave the change rooms and loop around the back of the Kent Pavilion before running through Nicholson's Arch – erected in honour of legendary College coach Skonk Nicholson.

There were many rugby traditions at College that had been in place for decades. In rugby season all College boys slept with their jersey under their pillows the night before every game. All the open age-group teams would meet at Clark House on a Friday night. We would polish our boots together and then trail down to Goldstones to 'the flick' – a ceremony which would see us all gather at the centre of Goldstones. The 1st XV captain would say some inspiring words, we'd have a big war cry, which was known as 'No 1', and then each team would leave the big circle, and make their own huddles. I would love to elaborate a bit more on what really goes on down there – but don't want to be responsible for any unnecessary inquiries, if you know what I mean. Let's just say it's a little College secret.

There was always a huge buzz around College on Friday nights before games. In a College change room you always put your jersey on last, because you needed to be ready before you pull that jersey over your head. The boots of every single player in the school were blackened out, and still are to this day. This is to prevent individuals from being too 'main' and fancying themselves.

It was also a great way of levelling out the rich and the poor. All our boots looked the same. It didn't matter if you had the best or worst boots. No one would know because that didn't matter, but it didn't stop the guys from always wanting the best.

Maritzburg College was the last of the big schools to get numbers on their 1st XV jerseys. This was because if you played for College you played for College. It didn't matter what number you were; numbers never existed, but team spirit did. However, the numbers were eventually added in 1998 because they were necessary for televised matches – and not without good reason. In my final year we played against Grey Bloem in a televised game and I was called Butch Lindsay by the commentator for the entire match because of the absence of numbers.

No account of rugby at Maritzburg College would be complete without paying due respect to the great Skonk Nicholson. Skonk is a name that goes hand in hand with College. He was the school's legendary master and coach and his fame was carried far beyond the confines of College.

Skonk, who passed away early in 2011 at the age of 94, was born James Mervyn Nicholson in Underberg, KwaZulu-Natal, on 6 February 1917. He grew up on the family farm and was sent to Durban Preparatory High School, after which he moved to Durban High School (DHS).

His father was a friend of the DHS headmaster and so he was sent to DHS rather than Maritzburg College. He enjoyed a successful stay in his few years at DHS and matriculated there in 1935 as head prefect. He captained the first team rugby and cricket sides and captained the Natal Schools rugby side.

It was as a young boarder at DHS that he earned his famous nickname 'Skonk'.

The head prefect at the time, M Bennett, responded to the young Nicholson's spirited nature and started calling him 'skonkwaan', the Zulu word for tent-peg or nail, and the abbreviation stuck for the rest of Skonk's life.

Skonk completed his tertiary education at the Natal University College in Pietermaritzburg and started out his academic teaching at DHS just before World War II had broken out.

He served as a sergeant major during the war before being released from duty due to injury. Skonk was then sent to Maritzburg College to teach.

He became the subject of a tug-of-war. The headmaster of College at the time was John Willie Hudson, a man of great personality. However, the headmaster of DHS, Colonel

Martin, wanted Skonk to be on his permanent staff and the education department sent Mr Hudson a letter instructing him to release Skonk to DHS. Mr Hudson apparently called Skonk in and said: 'Boy, I have a letter here saying you have to go to some school in Durban. You are not going, boy. You are a full-time member of the College staff!'

Skonk didn't go. He was sent to Maritzburg College for a six-month stint and stayed for 60 years. He taught geography and coached the 1st XV from 1948 to 1982. Quite amazing isn't it? That's 34 years of his life. Talk about dedication.

Under Skonk's leadership, College became one of South Africa's schoolboy rugby powerhouses. He produced 14 unbeaten 1st XVs, not to mention countless Natal Schools and SA Schools players during his 34 seasons as coach. Skonk built the success of his teams around fitness and the famous five Ps – Pace, Pride, Possession, Power, Position.

He always believed you should have at least one redhead in your team because he said it created 'fire in the belly'. Until the day of his passing, you'd see Skonk making his way down to Goldstones on a Saturday in one of his 1960s Valiants. He celebrated his 90th birthday on 6 February 2007 down on Goldstones. His guest of honour was his dear friend Ian McIntosh, the former Springbok and Natal Sharks coach, who spoke of the great debt he owed Skonk Nicholson, revealing how he had often confided in or sought advice from the great schoolboy mentor.

Skonk coached many other teams too. The late Dr Danie Craven even sent him as far as Chile and he also served as an SA Schools coach and selector. He coached club sides, including Collegians and DHS Old Boys of Durban and Old Collegians in Pietermaritzburg. Mac called him the Doc Craven of Natal rugby. May the legend and spirit of Skonk Nicholson live on forever at Maritzburg College.

Soon it was time to leave school and as with so many of my peers I had no idea what I wanted to do – other than play rugby that is. I hadn't played as much sport as I would have liked to because of my knee ops but I really did want to play for the College 1st XV, so I decided to do a post-matric.

There was a whole lot of controversy around the topic of post-matrics at the time. I believe there still is to a certain degree, but in the old days guys would fail on purpose to play another year of rugby. But I was young for my class so figured it was the right thing to do.

I also wasn't jumping ship. It was College or nothing. I was reminded the other day that once I finished my extra year I actually asked if I could do another year; I suppose you would call it a post, post-matric. In terms of age I was still eligible and besides, who wants to face the daunting reality of leaving your sport behind for what could be an office job? Needless to say the school declined my request.

This was the year I turned 18 and got my driver's licence. I've always had a huge passion for cars. My mom had one of the original Minis and it became my little hotrod. My party trick was to get into the passenger seat, keep my hands down low and put my legs across to reach the pedals to make it look as though there was no driver. I would act blasé as the car whizzed along and you should have seen people's faces as I passed, especially the old folk. Their eyes would be like saucers. It looked like the little Mini was driving itself!

One Sunday afternoon I had no fewer than seven girls in the Mini. We went to Wimpy for some ice cream and then returned to my house. My mom asked the girls how they all got there.

They told her that I had fetched them from school.

My mom flipped and told my dad. He came home and read me the riot act, but without too much conviction in his voice because I think he was quite impressed.

It was around this time we went out in Pietermaritzburg one night. On our way home the driver of our car, Kevin Deana, a feisty little character, got into an altercation with a tow truck driver. They started arguing about something while we were getting into the car. As you can imagine the rest of us were quite keen for Kevin to just leave the whole thing, as tow truck drivers are not known to be the friendliest of guys. A few nasty words were exchanged and we drove off, but we hadn't gone very far when we noticed that the tow truck driver was in pursuit. Out of sheer panic we ended up turning down a road, which was a dead end.

We all thought that this could very easily be the end for us. The road was right above the Duzi River in a deserted park and I had visions of us being shot and thrown in the river. So when these guys got out of the car, I made a beeline for it. My intention was to get some help for the boys. But what happened while I was away was that all the guys got sjambokked by the tow truck driver.

They started with Kevin and were giving him a good whipping when Slobby Muir, another mate of ours, shouted for them to stop. All that did was turn their attention to him and they gave him one across the face with the sjambok.

The boys had welts all over their bodies. They still give me gears for 'deserting' them that night. They spice up the story and always say that I ran shouting, 'Hey, I have a career to look after!' But I don't know, I think their ears were either clogged up with nerves or booze.

The funny thing about my post-matric year is that I started the rugby season in the 2nd XV but by the second game of the season I finally got my chance to turn out for the 1st XV. I was in and out of the team during the first half of the season but towards the latter half I had become a regular, which came with an excellent bonus as that meant I was in the squad for College's tour to the UK. But it also meant I had reached a crossroads. It was now time to make a decision as to which sport I was going to pursue, as the tour to the UK was at the same time as the Coca-Cola inter-provincial cricket week. I received a phone call from our cricket coach saying that I had a good chance of making the Natal Schools cricket side and wanted to know what I was going to do.

Tough question for a young guy so I said, 'Well, if I make the Natal A side I'll stay for the cricket, but if I make the B side I'll choose the rugby tour.'

As fate would have it I was chosen for the Natal B side. Deep down I was quite happy, though. We had been raising money for our rugby tour all year and I was really looking forward to it.

So rugby got the nod and it would be true to say that going on tour changed the course of my life.

3

THE STORY OF THE BIG HIT

Maritzburg College's tour to the UK was hugely successful. We played all the top schools in the UK and dominated in a big way, winning all our games convincingly while having a lot of fun off the field.

As you can imagine, it would be really difficult for a group of 25 schoolboys (most of whom had just matriculated) not to get up to some high jinks on a tour like this and once again the word 'naughty' comes to mind. On one occasion we were rebuked by one of the hosting schools' headmasters. Some of the schools we played against were co-ed, the boys were billeted by local families and some of the lucky buggers ended up with families who had really attractive daughters. Need I say more?

One of the guys on that tour was Chad Erskine, who went on to represent the USA Eagles in the 2007 World Cup. Chad was a huge Jeremy Guscott fan and a Bath RFC fanatic. When we passed through Bath, Chad decided to splash out his pocket money on what seemed like half of the supporters' club memorabilia. Jerseys, socks, tracksuits, jocks, you name it … if there was something to buy in that shop he bought it. And if that wasn't enough, he had the England rose tattooed on his buttocks! You can imagine the reaction of our coaches. Chad had a year left at school so he took a bit of flak for getting that tattoo. And would you believe that I was the one who ended up at Bath?

The course of my life took a turn on this tour. For some reason I just came into my own and played some really good rugby. I think I had grown a bit in the year and I had a lot of confidence. Our coach Mr Colin Heard – who we referred to as 'Tick' or 'Tokolosh' – was really impressed with my game and at the end of the year paid me a compliment in the College yearbook by saying that if I had shown my tour form for the whole of the season he would have pushed for me to don the No 10 jersey in the Natal Schools side as I had been the best schoolboy flyhalf with whom he had worked.

It turned out to be fortuitous for me that Mr Heard was leaving Maritzburg College to take up a position at the Natal Rugby Union. His parting words to me were that I should really give my rugby a go and that he would be looking out for me.

On returning to South Africa most of the boys struck out in their separate directions. Many went down to the Cape, to either study or play rugby for Ikeys at the University of Cape Town or for Maties at Stellenbosch University. I didn't have any clear idea of what I wanted to do with my life and because I loved sport so much I decided that a post-matric, a part-time job at Jackson Sports in Pietermaritzburg and playing rugby would suit me just fine.

Elton was playing for Collegians Wasps so I would spend many a Friday night or Saturday, when I didn't have rugby commitments of my own, watching him play.

Watching Elton put in such good performances but get so little recognition because he was based in Pietermaritzburg prompted me to make an effort to play my rugby in Durban. It was clear to me that if I wanted to get anywhere I was going to have to play for a Durban-based club. Elton, who moved to Stellenbosch later on to study and play rugby for Maties, did play for the Natal U21 side, but I felt he should have played for the senior side and that he was being overlooked because he was based in Maritzburg.

I was like a little kid when Elton used to get his Natal kit. I would sometimes wait up late at night just to see him arrive home and go through his new black and white gear. I was extremely proud watching Elton play at Kings Park and it inspired me to the point of making up my mind about what I wanted to achieve. Sitting in the stands at Kings Park, I thought to myself: 'This is what I want to do. This is where I want to play.'

I decided to sign up with College Rovers, situated in the lee of the Kings Park stadium, and started my crazy routine of driving from Pietermaritzburg to Durban for rugby practices. That's a 200km round trip per practice. And who would join me in this crazy escapade? None other than Peter Cameron – my partner in crime from way back. Pete and I had come through the ranks together at Merchiston and College and our next adventure was to take on Durban.

My dad would drive us down a lot of the time, as he knew how important it was to me; Pete would also drive on the odd occasion and if both those options fell through I would jump behind the wheel of my mom's old Mini. God alone knows how that jalopy made it there and back. If you're familiar with the drive, you'll know that it's not exactly a flat road – the hills come thick and fast. One thing that worked in our favour was the fact that Pete's dad had a petrol station and we used to fill up the car for free – thus enabling us to keep the money College Rovers gave us as 'danger pay'.

I worked at Jackson Sports during the day, travelled to practices in Durban twice a week and then back again for games. That's about 600km a week to chase an odd-shaped ball around. Some would call it madness but for me it was a lot of fun.

I had chosen to play my rugby for Berea Rovers (to give the club its old name) because of its strong association with Maritzburg College. Most College boys who lived in Durban joined Rovers. They were kind enough to give me some money towards petrol, were a great club to play for and provided the perfect launch pad for my leap from the juniors to the seniors.

When I joined Rovers to play for the U21 side, former College boys who were 'heavies' at the club included Geoff Appleford, Pieter Dixon and Trevor 'Benny' Boynton. It was good to have some familiar faces around and it added to the camaraderie that made playing for Rovers so much fun. There was a great vibe among all the guys who played for the club, on and off the field.

Rovers was founded in 1899 as Durban Rugby Club. Strangely enough, up until that date Durban's only winter sport had been soccer, which was in total contrast to Pietermaritzburg, where rugby had been established as a competitive sport since 1890, with its clubs challenging for the Murray Cup – an ornate silver trophy that had been donated by Sir TK Murray, the first president of the Natal Rugby Union.

Durban Rovers could not have made a more impressive start to life as a rugby club as they stunned the local rugby fraternity by winning the Murray Cup in their first year.

In 1936 Rovers amalgamated with Berea Cricket Club, which had been founded in 1885. The club became known as Berea Rovers Sports Club – the oldest sports club of its kind in KwaZulu-Natal and one of the oldest in the country.

Rovers boast an impressive honours board on which the names of 22 Springboks are listed – including two captains in Gary Teichmann and the late Roy Dryburgh.

Rovers also produced a Springbok Sevens captain in Marc de Marigny and two Springbok coaches in Cecil Moss and Ian McIntosh – who was the first coach to lead a Natal side to Currie Cup glory. Needless to say his captain was a Maritzburg College and Rovers old boy – Craig Jamieson.

Other Rovers Springboks include Guy Kebble, James Small, Pieter Müller, Robbie Kempson, Joel Stransky, Jeremy Thomson, Toks van der Linde, Chris Rossouw, Gaffie du Toit, Dave von Hoesslin, AJ Venter and Stefan Terblanche, and more recently Ryan Kankowski and Keegan Daniel.

One of my earliest memories of club rugby is a Rovers tour to Bloemfontein. We went up there to play against Old Grey and in the great tradition of club rugby a few of the guys went out and painted Bloem all shades of red. I recall one of the Rovers coaching staff getting so hammered on that tour that he actually shat in his pants. I know it sounds really disgusting, and I apologise, but that's what happened! That's club rugby for you. Some are there for the boozing, some are there for the boozing and the rugby, while others are there purely for the rugby.

While on the same tour, a guy by the name of John Haynes went out and got so tanked up that he rocked up at the match the next day still in his jeans and casual shirt, probably after having had an all-nighter. If no one had said anything he probably would have run on to the field in his jeans.

One night a few of us ended up mingling with a few girls from Bloem. We got them to give us a lift back to where we were staying – a place that was infested by mosquitoes – and things started getting a bit mischievous with the boys taking the chance to practise their 'handling skills'. But the fun came to an abrupt end when we were suddenly T-boned by another car. That brought an end to any roaming hands in the car and luckily no one was badly injured. The girls were in a bit of shock, the evening was at an end and we had to be collected and taken back to the mosquito nest to sleep it off.

Looking back now, driving between Pietermaritzburg and Durban for practices and games seems like a pain, but I really enjoyed that time of my life. It was a carefree, fun time but things became a bit more serious when I made the Natal U21 side.

Rugby union was just edging towards professionalism and I was paid R500 a game. It might seem like peanuts now but to me it was a handsome sum. I grew up with little money around so R500 for doing what I loved was pretty nifty.

The travelling eventually came to be a bit trying for my dad and me. While I was living my dream, it must have been a chore for him, but he never complained. It was just one of the many things my mom and dad did to help my rugby career along.

Eventually the rugby commute had to stop and to be quite honest, I could no longer resist the Durban lifestyle. It was time to pack my bags and relocate to 'Durbs'.

As I mentioned, there were a few old Collegians at Rovers and Trevor 'Benny' Boynton, who is a legend in his own right for putting in some big hits in his day, had become good mates with a guy by the name of John Smit, who came from Pretoria Boys' High. They met while playing together for Natal U21 and it was through Benny and playing at Rovers that I became close friends with John. Having moved down to Durban, I was looking for digs so John and I moved in together. Sean Cooper also lived with us and we were later joined by Chris Pearson. There was also an outside room – so Mr Peter Cameron claimed his place there.

John and I would end up playing quite a bit of rugby together, even though he moved through the ranks quicker than I did. I played some good rugby at Rovers and was really chuffed when I made the Natal U21 side. Our coach was a man by the name of Swys de Bruin. He was a former teacher and a good coach, but it was certainly evident that he had been a school master. His methods were quite strict;

he didn't like things like swearing at all and that certainly made it hard for guys like Craig Davidson and co.

Running on to Kings Park was a dream come true. My Natal U21 debut was against Transvaal at Ellis Park. I played flyhalf that game, but was then shifted to inside centre as Swys had opted to go with a guy by the name of Jaco van der Westhuyzen at flyhalf. Yes – the same Jaco van der Westhuyzen who played for the Boks and the Bulls. Yes, the guy who clambered up the posts at Kings Park after the Super 14 final in 2007 to gesticulate triumphantly to the crowd before ripping off his blue jersey to reveal a T-shirt bearing a religious message.

It was around this time that I started putting in those big hits. I wasn't a good defender at school. I wouldn't say I was weak on defence, but it certainly wasn't something I prided myself on. But one Friday night during a club game between DHS Old Boys and Rovers I changed my game and style of playing rugby forever, without even realising it. From that night on the main characteristic of my game would become fierce, harsh, uncompromising tackling. The story behind all of this was quite simple really and I didn't realise the significance of a single tackle I put in that night.

What happened was that my girlfriend and I had broken up. It had been a really terrible week for me and I had built up a lot of anger, so I was on edge as we ran on to the field. I wouldn't say I was having an extraordinary game, but near the end, one of the DHS Old Boys forwards broke through and I found myself as the last defender. So I just lined him up and flew into him with everything I had.

I cleaned him up so hard that he lay writhing on the ground; I think he was then taken off on a stretcher. My mates on the touchline made a huge racket and the small but vocal crowd let me know how much they approved of and loved that hit. That's how it all started and once you get that feeling you can't go without it. I simply grew to love tackling and to this day it's a part of the game I really look forward to.

I had always looked up to Henry Honiball as a youngster and loved the way he played, especially the way he used to make opposing flyhalves jittery because they knew what was in store. I also noticed how the flyhalves representing Australia and New Zealand at the time – Stephen Larkham for instance – never really got going when 'Lem' (Blade) was in the Bok No 10 jersey.

Flyhalves don't particularly like getting hit hard and I realised there was an advantage to be had by shaking them up. I enjoyed putting in a big hit or two. After Lem, our flyhalves in South Africa were not known for strong defence and that gave the New Zealanders and other strong teams a lot of freedom in the channel. Lem was a hero of mine and my aim was to try and instil the kind of fear that he did.

So there you have it. One tackle in a minor game on a back field in Durban one night transformed my game. The ability to put in big hits would get me a place in the starting line-up for the Sharks and add so much to my style of play, but it would also get me into a lot of trouble.

I played for the Natal U21 side for a year or two and was fortunate enough to make the South Africa U21 side two years in a row; the first under a young coach by the name of Jake White. I spent a lot of time on the bench in my first year with the Baby Boks as Jaco van der Westhuyzen was the first-choice flyhalf. In 1999 we went to Argentina to play in the Sanzar/UAR U21 Championship, the precursor to what would become the U21 World Cup. We had a strong team and went on to win the tournament with John as captain; interestingly enough playing at tighthead prop.

I wasn't in the starting team for the final but it was filled with names you might recognise: Johan Roets, Wylie Human, De Wet Barry, Wayne Julies, Frikkie Welsh, Jaco van der Westhuyzen, Shaun Sowerby, Gerrie Britz, Hendro

Scholtz, John Smit, Skipper Badenhorst, Lawrence Sephaka and a big Bishops boy who went on to play Test match rugby for the Wallabies, Daniel Vickerman.

The Baby Blacks weren't too shy either. Ben Blair, Doug Howlett, Rico Gear, Jerry Collins, Chris Jack, Paul Tito and Carl Hayman were some of the guys we were up against in the final. We won 27-25 after Frikkie Welsh had scored a try in the very last movement of the game and Johan Roets had landed the match-winning conversion.

The next year we went to New Zealand for what was by then the U21 World Cup. André Pretorius and I shared the flyhalf duties. However, I played most of the games at centre as the coach wanted to introduce my defence into the mix. We were a good side, captained by Wikus van Heerden, but were beaten in the final by a stronger New Zealand team. Both teams also included a number of players who would become household names in the ensuing years and the precedent had been established that when it came to selecting AD James for any rugby side, tackling would be a strong consideration.

4

A HEART LIKE A SHARK

Schooldays were soon forgotten as I settled into Durban's relaxed lifestyle. I had made some good friends, the rugby scene was great and the Natal Sharks were on the up thanks to an outstanding coaching staff, not to mention excellent support from their sponsors. Alistair McArthur and his team at Mr Price were, and continue to be, absolutely phenomenal in their commitment to Natal rugby. Hats off to them.

The social life in Durban was certainly better than in Pietermaritzburg. I immediately loved living in Durban and I still do. The climate is great, the people are really friendly and down-to-earth, there are good restaurants – the aptly-named Butcher Boys probably being my favourite – and above all, it's pretty laid-back, which suits me perfectly.

The set-up at the Natal Rugby Union was excellent and I bought into the culture big time. These were the days before I learned of the pressure accompanying big games for the Springboks and the Sharks. I was young, up-and-coming, with nothing to lose and living a life most only dream of.

It was a period in which I was getting a feel for playing rugby full time, getting to taste a bit of the Sharks' and Baby Boks' cultures and I liked the taste. A lot.

The Natal Rugby Union was founded in 1890 but its team did not appear in a Currie Cup final until the 1956 season when they played Northern Transvaal (later to become the Blue Bulls) at the home of Natal rugby, Kings Park, but were denied what would have been a famous victory as they went down 8-9.

Next, captained by Wynand Claassen and coached by Roger Gardner, Natal made the final in 1984 but once again victory eluded the 'Banana Boys' as they went down 9-19 to Western Province at Newlands.

However, the arrival of Ian McIntosh as coach signalled the advent of a golden era for Natal rugby. The union's centenary was in 1990 and there was determination in the air to celebrate 100 years of rugby in the province Tommy Bedford famously called 'the last outpost of the British Empire' with something really special.

'Mr Mac' had put together a mighty pack of forwards, imposed his belief in direct rugby and Natal won through to oppose Northern Transvaal in the 1990 Currie Cup final at Loftus Versfeld in Pretoria.

And finally all of Natal could celebrate as the team clinched an epic 18-12 victory. Natal won the game courtesy of wing Tony Watson's famous nine-point try. With the score at 12-9 Watson shrugged off Theo van Rensburg's attempted tackle before sprinting clear and wheeling around to score behind the posts. That made the score 13-12 (four-point tries in those days) in Natal's favour with the conversion to come.

Joel Stransky, sporting a bandage because of a cut to the head, converted to give Natal a three-point lead and then returned to the centre spot to attempt a penalty – the result of Watson having been fouled by Northern Transvaal centre Jannie Claassens as he skidded in for his try. Joel raised the flags with the penalty to stretch the score to 18-12 and the biggest party ever seen in the territory east of the Drakensberg was just minutes away.

The victorious Natal side was led by Craig Jamieson. He was a real terrier and always played with his socks around his ankles. He was scruffy – but tough.

I recall how stoked the whole of Natal was when we won the cup. It was as if a curse had been lifted off the union and its supporters and would herald a period under Ian McIntosh in which Natal, soon to be renamed the Sharks, would come to be called the Team of the '90s.

Mac was a stern guy but a great coach. It's true to say he pulled Natal rugby out of the doldrums. He engendered a winning culture and *gees* (a great Afrikaans word denoting a bit more than just spirit) into Natal rugby. A true legend.

Mac never minced his words. On one occasion he asked a young Shaun Sowerby at his first Sharks practice, 'What's your name c**t?' Shaun stammered his name, to which Mac replied, 'Ja, I've heard about you. This is your first practice, make sure it's not your last.' That was Mac for you; straight, tough and to the point, but he knew what he wanted from his team and how to get them there.

My rugby, meanwhile, was progressing well. I was getting into the Natal Wildebeest mix, which is like a Sharks B side, and another tour presented itself – a Wildebeest excursion to Wales. It was an awesome tour on and off the field. We played well, at a rate of two games a week, and had a lot of fun. Some guys got quite loose on that trip … but naturally only once the business end of the day had been handled.

As always there were a few clowns; Craig Davidson and Shaun for instance. They got hooked on playing 'last touch' with each other and, as 20-year-olds on a rugby tour would do, took it to extremes. Craig even slept outside Shaun's door one night to get him. Ridiculous! It reached a low point after a particularly rough night on the town.

Craig had got a run at scrummie and played out of his boots, so I suppose he felt bulletproof. It was last touch here, last touch there and the rest of us laughed them off and hit the sack. Next morning most of the team were having breakfast and in comes Craig with a severely swollen and clearly broken nose. What had happened was that he had last-touched Shaun and turned to sprint away only to smash headlong into a corner in the corridor. Fool.

Craig is a great guy and one of my best mates. We played some good rugby together, climbing the Natal ranks as a halfback combination. He really was a great scrummie to play behind; he had a heart like a lion and was unselfish. He would rarely release scrappy ball to me and sadly had to pull the plug on his rugby career a lot earlier than he wanted to after several bouts of concussion, which were often caused by his fearless approach to the game.

It may sound as though I was on a carefree ride but it was around this time that the flame started burning in me. It was the first time in my life that I started to think that something bigger and better was on the cards for me – that I could lead an extraordinary life through rugby.

John Smit and I rented a flat together after moving on from the previous digs and when John decided to buy a house, Shaun and I moved in too. We spent many memorable years there together.

John's talent was recognised early on. He was deep in the Sharks' mix and became a Springbok at an early age but things were also happening for me in terms of the Natal senior provincial side.

There were a few other guys in the senior side running in the No 10 jersey, but I was quietly growing in confidence and starting to get really focused in spite of a quick turnaround of coaches at the Sharks.

Hugh Reece-Edwards took over from Mac at the end of '99; quickly followed by Rudolf Straeuli, a member of the

'95 World Cup-winning Springbok side; and then Kevin Putt, when Straeuli was given the Bok coaching job.

My big break came when Rudolf, in response to a poor Super 12 performance the previous year, organised trials. I knew that if I made an impact the door to the Natal senior side might open, so I flew into a few guys and made some really big hits. I think it was the kind of fire Rudolf was looking for in the flyhalf channel. My distribution and all-round game was also good and the B team, for which I was playing, pulled off a draw against the Super 12 side.

My timing couldn't have been better. Natal were battling to fill the void left by Henry Honiball and had tried a few options at flyhalf that hadn't really worked. Natal play well when they are physical and in the opponents' faces, so my robust style caught the eye of the coaches.

I was selected as first-choice flyhalf, ahead of guys like Gaffie du Toit and Clinton van Rensburg, and played at No 10 for the Sharks for the entire 2000 Currie Cup season. When I received my first call-up I recall sitting on the bench with Gary Teichmann. I think he was coming back from an injury and you can imagine what an impression it made on me to be playing alongside some Sharks legends and some of my schoolboy heroes at such a young age.

The senior guys in the Sharks set-up were great. They brought us youngsters through well – but in an old school, unsympathetic sort of way. Mark Andrews was a classic example. He really looked after the younger guys. You always knew Mark had your back if you played in the same team as him. He was really cool in a gruff sort of way. He wasn't friendly to you, but he always made sure you were OK and I respected him for that.

I loved playing with Mark. He didn't do too much talking – but he used to discipline the guys on the field and put in some hard hits. He played the game with a lot of fire and passion. And when you saw guys like Mark putting their bodies on the line you'd follow suit and also start flying into guys. I was once standing at a ruck and Mark came flying in. He dislocated his finger really badly. He took one look at it, decided he couldn't wait for the medics, forced it back in to place himself and got on with the game. After the match it turned out the finger was actually broken. That was Mark Andrews, one tough bugger. He played the next two games in spite of that broken finger. Mark wrote me an awesome letter when he retired which really touched me because it was not something he did for everyone.

Another guy who always looked after me was AJ Venter. He and Mark were always passing on invaluable knowledge to me and giving me plenty of sound advice. I think I was accepted by the older boys in the forwards because they liked having a flyhalf who gave his all and defended his channel.

I had started making a reputation for myself. I was solid on defence and I was blessed with the ability to distribute the ball with speed and accuracy to both sides. It's a part of my game I have always prided myself on. Good hands. Too often the critics failed to notice that aspect of my game. Once on a night out after a Sharks game a girl told me I had good hands. I joked that I hadn't dropped a ball since mini-rugby and still wonder whether that was the right reply.

Rugby was rapidly becoming a serious part of my life. For those first few years in the senior side I hardly went out socialising during the week. It was quite a sacrifice because many of my mates were at varsity and they were going out all the time. Boozing, chasing skirt, doing what most normal young guys have always done. However, something drove me to remain focused to get to where I wanted to be. I lost contact with quite a few friends but I suppose that comes with the territory. For the first few years at Natal it was just Natal rugby, Natal rugby and more Natal rugby.

The Natal aficionados appreciated the way I approached my game. And the supporters started taking to my style too as they had been waiting for a successor to Henry Honiball to make his appearance.

I loved playing rugby at Kings Park – also known as the Shark Tank. I was feeling more and more comfortable in the black and white No 10 jersey. That field was my terrain in which I could patrol as a lethal predator. My heart and mind were operating more and more like a Shark in stealth mode. It was becoming instinct.

5

LOOK MA, NO ARMS

he Sharks were in good shape in the lead-up to the 2001 Super 12. We had put in some severe pre-season training and the guys in the camp were motivated to do well and restore pride. There was a nice mix of old and new in the make-up of the squad and as one of the new boys I wanted to make a mark. It was to be my introduction to the big time.

Super Rugby is no place for the faint-hearted. If you hesitate out there you're dead. There are some really big collisions, huge tackles and it's played at a brutal pace.

We had put in the graft, and it was now time to get stuck in and produce the goods. I was pretty young but it worked in my favour, because I was more than hungry and had youthful exuberance on my side.

The Polynesian Islanders (Maori, Samoans, Fijians and Tongans) are notorious for their aggressive tackling, so I thought they'd really appreciate it if I returned the favour! I was like a scud missile out there, putting in big hits game after game. If the ball came out to the opposition it was as if a button had been pressed and I went into tackle mode. I just loved it.

I don't know if it took people by surprise to see a flyhalf making such physical hits, but my tackling antics sparked an outcry during our away tour to New Zealand and Australia. The powers that be started zeroing in on me and the media got on my case, but I felt there was respect from the public for the role I was performing. The funny thing is that I started getting nailed by my own people; it felt bizarre. The Kiwis and Aussies never started the inquest into the whole 'Butch James – no arms' saga. It was back in South Africa where it got out of hand.

I felt my debut Super 12 season had gone well. I grew in confidence and my game really spiked. I was on a roll and it felt as if I had found real form. There was quite a lot of praise too; here was this new kid on the block who was putting in huge hits and could distribute the ball better and quicker than most. It was important in the bigger scheme of things, because if I hadn't made the adjustment to Super 12, if I'd cracked, then I might have blown my chance for good.

The fact that I'd made an impact and played well meant a lot to me. And it wasn't just the tackling. My distribution was sound and my kicking game was much improved; I had come on in leaps and bounds in a very short space of time. My vision for the game had clicked in, thanks in large part to the coaching staff at the Sharks who put a lot of hard work into developing my game.

I couldn't have been doing too badly; the Sharks made the Super 12 final thanks to a massive team effort. The forwards dominated and secured good ball for the backs, which paid off. We met the ACT Brumbies in the final in Canberra, but were beaten by a better side on the day.

I obviously had a lot to learn but my all-round game had something good going for it and I was rewarded by being called up to Harry Viljoen's Springbok squad to make my debut against France in June. It is the biggest honour that can be bestowed on a youngster playing rugby in South Africa and for me it was a dream come true, but the call-up to the Boks caught me by surprise, partly because I was so wrapped up in trying to play well week in and week out for the Sharks that I never really had too much time to think about being chosen for the national side, and because of the bizarre way I learned of my selection.

Becoming a Springbok was a huge ambition of mine but at that point I had played only one full Currie Cup season followed by the Super 12, so when I heard the news I was thrilled but also a little blind-sided.

Joost van der Westhuizen was at scrumhalf and there were a few other legends in the set-up. Joost was obviously a great No 9 but I don't think our styles gelled that well. Test rugby was a new experience and I got a harsh wake-up call as to just how small the margin is between winning and losing.

During this 2001 season I hurt my knee in a Test against Australia. I felt my knee jump out of place slightly during the game but played on. Back in Durban I was referred to Durban-based orthopaedic surgeon Dr Jaco Willers, who after performing an MRI scan, diagnosed a grade one tear to my LCL (lateral collateral ligament), with defects to the surface of my cartilage as well as some bone bruising. It was suggested that I be treated conservatively – which means trying everything other than the extreme route of operating. That meant a knee brace, but fortunately I recovered well and was playing again after a few weeks.

After the Bok fixtures we went straight in to the Currie Cup. On a whole it was a year in which I grew tremendously as a player. My mindset had gone up a few gears, but my defensive style would prove to be very costly. We were playing against the Free State Cheetahs and an official cited me for three 'dangerous' tackles. Once again all the talk was of Butch James not using his arms properly. Yawn.

It seemed as if the speed cops of rugby were determined to put me away in prison for life for not using my arms. I really felt as though they were out to get me – especially when I copped an eight-week suspension.

That's two whole months for not getting my forearms around a guy in the tackle. At least penalise me for going in dangerously with the shoulder or dangerously high. I've seen guys who blatantly throw punches or stomp on people who don't even get eight weeks!

I don't intend to get into the nitty-gritty of this and I'm certainly not going to dissect every tackle I put in. Yes, some of them may have looked a bit suspect and could have been executed in a neater fashion. But eight weeks? Please. That's like expelling a kid from school for being late for class.

I also knew when I was on the edge but let me tell you, the officials were clueless because what amazed me was that they often called the wrong ones. I would put in a great tackle and get nailed for it, then I'd put in a tackle and think 'Jeez, they're going to zero in on me for that one, I'm definitely going off,' but they'd let it slide. It was quite ridiculous.

Refs were even coming up to me in the tunnel as we were about to run on and saying: 'No 10 – we are watching you. No tackling without the arms please. If I see a bad tackle, you're off.' It used to get under my skin. I think every player deserves to go into a new game with a clean slate. Every game is a new one. If you do something in that game, then fine, hand out the punishment. But this issue was dragging out and was spilling over from one game to another.

Rudolf Straeuli backed me and insisted that I shouldn't change my style, perhaps be a bit more careful, but he wanted me to play my game. I never put in a hit that directly cost us a game and I reckon aggressive tackling is part of rugby. Putting in big hits was what I thrived on and in many ways was what counted in my favour when coaches sat down to select teams. I had no choice but to take my eight weeks on the chin, but as you can imagine, I was not happy. It meant missing a big part of the season. But every cloud has a silver lining and the banning happened to coincide with what had become a chronic problem with my right knee. So I thought it would be a great time to get my knee checked out.

The knee was quite unstable and I was worried because this was the one on which I had a surgical reconstruction of my ACL (anterior cruciate ligament) back in 1996 while still at school. I flew to Johannesburg to see Dr Mark Ferguson at the Rosebank Centre for Sports Medicine to get the knee checked out. I had eight weeks to play with and was hoping it would be nothing too serious, perhaps a bit of cartilage that needed cleaning out. A cartilage op can take a few weeks to heal whereas ligament repair takes much longer.

My knee was swollen and they needed to drain it – which is when you can tell if it's cartilage or ligaments. When the doctor sucks the fluid out it should come out a sort of whisky colour, but as it appeared in the catheter it looked red and I knew straight away that it was ligaments. You didn't need to tell me what this meant and I was shattered. That was the start of my long haul with knee problems; injuries that to a great extent would dictate the course of my career.

Dr Ferguson examined me and confirmed looseness of the cartilage as well as some extra damage to the articular cartilage or lining of the joint. We had a lengthy discussion on the need for further surgery and the impact it would have on my rugby career. I had a huge sinking feeling in my heart. The combination of a failed ACL and now permanent damage to the joint was a huge setback as the success after revisionary surgery would never be as good as the first op.

You can imagine how down I felt when Dr Ferguson told me he could not guarantee how much longer I would be able to play rugby.

I couldn't believe my luck. I was young, I had just made the Springboks, played six games for the green and gold and now it was all about to be ripped away. There was talk of building for the 2003 Rugby World Cup in Australia and in a country like South Africa competition to get a place in the Bok side is stiff. Things change very quickly and it takes a hell of a lot to get back into your game after having a knee op, but as they say in those direct mail ads – there was more to come. It was to be my second experience of knee surgery. However, I had four more operations to go – I just didn't know it yet.

Fortunately for me I've always had a default button marked 'Optimism' so I switched into fightback mode. We decided to go ahead with the surgery, which was done the same day. Arthroscopy (placing a camera in the joint through small holes) showed that I had retorn the ACL and had some articular damage right down to my bone. Dr Ferguson used two double strands of my hamstring to reconstruct my ACL and tried to stimulate some cartilage regrowth in the area where it was damaged. Although the knee was now stable, the doc was very unsure as to what extent the cartilage would break down over time, but in the end the op was as much of a success as could be expected.

I returned to the Sharks' medical staff, who managed my rehabilitation and got me back on track. It was painful and I had to walk a windy, rocky road to recovery. It's a cruel thing to have had a taste of what Test rugby is about and then have to sit with crutches in your living room watching the Springboks run out on to the field.

But I was determined to play for the Sharks and the Boks again and the magical qualities of this dream helped me to make what was termed a miraculous recovery. By 2002 I was back on the field.

6

BECOMING
A BOK

Being chosen for the Springboks was amazing and gave me a lot of motivation to bounce back throughout the difficult stages of my career. It instilled a tremendous amount of pride and as you can imagine, being part of the Springbok family is far bigger than any individual accolade. For me it was the ultimate; a very special thing to be part of. The jersey is not yours, it is borrowed; to be cherished and worn with pride and commitment before being passed on to the next generation. You have to conduct yourself with the best interests of the Springboks at heart.

Becoming a Bok is such an enormous moment in a South African rugby player's life that it stands out forever, which makes the way I found out about my selection odd to say the least. We were playing a Super 12 game against the Stormers in Wellington and managed to sneak a win in the most extraordinary way. Stormers centre Robbie Fleck was put clean through and looked as though he would score a certain try but made the mistake of easing up to start enjoying the applause, only to be caught from behind by Deon Kayser. Deon proved the old adage that you must never give up and his tackle caused Robbie to lose the ball and cough up the try. Never a dull moment with Fleckie around!

We trooped off the field and the next thing SuperSport's Andy Capostagno grabbed me for an interview. I thought he was going to ask me about Fleckie's howler but instead he asked me if I was happy that I had been included in the Springbok squad. Just like that.

It was all very weird and was the last thing I was expecting to happen. There was no tension in having to wait in front of the TV, no excited phone calls. A simple question from Andy and that was that. I was a Bok.

It only started to hit me the next day; 'I am a Springbok', and it felt amazing. All those years of ball games, of being obsessed with sport; the seeming madness of pursuing a career in rugby had paid off. I felt privileged and enjoyed the moment with my family, who were extremely proud. That made it even better; it was payback for the effort and sacrifices my mom and dad had made for me.

Harry Viljoen had been appointed Bok coach and my debut would come against France at Ellis Park. Elton was based in London at the time and caught the first flight back to South Africa to be there for my debut. The whole Bok culture is something sacred and special. Running out to represent the Springboks for the first time sends shivers up the old spinal cord. Even though we lost 23-32, it was a special day for me.

The next game was also against the French – at Kings Park, my happy hunting ground. I kicked five penalty goals and we emerged victorious, 20-15. But in typical Butchie fashion there was a sting in the tail when I was cited for – you guessed it – an alleged 'no arms' tackle on France winger David Bory.

The disciplinary hearing took place directly after the game and I acted like a bit of a brat during proceedings because my folks, Elton and some close friends were on the outer fields having a braai and I couldn't wait to join them. It was my first hearing and I hadn't realised how long they actually take, so my impatience and naivety got the better of me. Looking back, I was probably lucky to have got just a week.

I missed the next match against Italy, but was back in the mix for the 2001 Tri-Nations and ended up starting every game in that series. We had an average tournament and only managed one win, 20-15, against Australia at Loftus Versfeld. The games were tight, though. We lost 3-12 to New Zealand at Newlands, then drew 14-14 with the Wallabies, who were No 1 in the world, at the Subiaco Oval in Perth.

There was quite a bit of drama in the Bok camp during this time. The captaincy was taken away from André Vos and passed to Bob Skinstad. Harry had a very different way of approaching things; he was the first coach to implement the new reality that rugby had become a profession. His approach was like that of the managers of big football sides overseas and he wasn't scared to bring in a plethora of experienced, specialised people to take on different roles. He would stand back and co-ordinate the process.

At our first kitting-out session Harry sent a lot of the clothing back and asked Woolworths to replace it with more modern, stylish outfits – hip leather coats and jeans that caused quite a stir when we first wore them. Harry felt that if we looked good and felt good, we would play good too. It was very different to what the senior guys were used to but I was of a newer generation and enjoyed this approach.

My first real memory of the Springboks was during the New Zealand Cavaliers tour in 1986. The Springboks won an action-packed series with legendary Boks such as Uli Schmidt, Naas Botha, Danie Gerber and Carel du Plessis in the mix. Boy, those guys had natural talent and flair.

In 1990 the first steps were taken to unban the ANC, release Nelson Mandela from prison and to start dismantling the legal apparatus of apartheid. One of the outcomes was that South African sportsmen were readmitted to international competition; the Springboks played Tests against the All Blacks and the Wallabies in South Africa followed by a tour to France and the UK in 1992. I was just edging into my teens when all this was happening but the excitement of playing the All Blacks again registered with all us 'pikkies' kicking a ball around in Pietermaritzburg.

Historically the term 'Springbok' was applied to any team or individual representing South Africa in international competition – regardless of the sport. This tradition was abandoned when the ANC government came into power after South Africa's first democratic elections in 1994, but thanks to Madiba's influence (Madiba is the affectionate name by which former president Nelson Mandela is known) there was a special dispensation that South African rugby could retain the Springbok as its emblem.

It was a masterstroke by Mandela, taken at considerable personal political risk, but the Springboks repaid his faith by winning the Rugby World Cup against all odds in 1995. People of all races and walks of life were proud to be South African, and seeing how Springbok rugby transcended race, culture, colour or beliefs made me doubly proud when I became one myself.

I take a great amount of interest in South Africa's history. It is a part of me and played a big role in shaping my life. You only get one crack at writing a book about your life and where you come from, so the historical content is fitting. Things change and in time no one will care about some of the things that played a part in my life. Who knows – Maritzburg College might not exist in 50 years' time. The Springbok emblem and all its history might also come to an end so I felt it was important to give some context to how one guy who loved his sport ended up being a Springbok and playing in two Rugby World Cups.

Speaking of knowledge, as a youngster I always wondered, as many of you do too I'm sure, what happens behind the scenes in the Springbok camp. What happens on the morning of a Test, or in the change room before a game?

I'll try to give you a feel for a week in the life of a Bok ahead of a Test match. The nerves are obviously there; it's mental urgency to the max. Monday, Tuesday and Wednesday go quite quickly, because you are so caught up in preparation and practice. From Thursday the time drags and all you want is for the game to arrive.

But then it picks up a bit. Friday is quite a *lekker* day; it's special in that you get your Springbok jersey. That happens at about 10am and usually involves a prominent person or a former Bok, who is invited to say a few words and do the presentation. Then we have the team photo, eat lunch, followed by what is called 'the captain's run' at whatever time our kick-off is the next day. We do a couple of runs through our set phases, go through some moves and then I'll do some kicking practice along with the other designated kickers. On Friday nights the guys tend to take it quite easy. I normally lie in my room and watch TV until I feel tired and fall asleep. At first I used to be extremely nervous and would battle to get to sleep but the more Tests I played the more comfortable I got. I think it's a case of each to himself. Some guys handle it well, while others get really on edge.

Most of us don't get up too early. Breakfast is between 8am and 10am. Guys like Schalk Burger wake up at one minute to 10. Some guys even miss breakfast – it's not compulsory.

Everyone reacts differently to the pressure of a looming Test match. If it's your first Test you probably won't be able to keep your food down anyway. Although our meals are carefully planned with the aid of a nutritionist we don't have individual diets to follow. In fact, the menu is quite flexible: no junk food, just a healthy spread of wholesome food to give the old engine the necessary fuel it needs to perform.

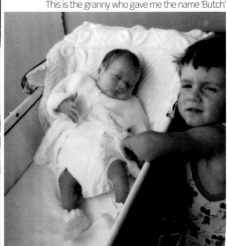

Opposite page (clockwise from top left): My first bicycle from Father Christmas; Elton and me showing off our Christmas presents; I always loved playing in the mud and getting dirty as a youngster; Elton and me camping in the back garden. Check Eltie's Walkman!; I have never been comfortable on a horse
This page (clockwise from top): My first year of school at Beaumont Primary; Eltie and me off to our first day of school for the year, with my dad in tow; sleeping on the stairs of our caravan, after going missing

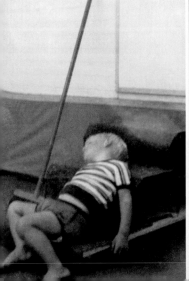

Butchie Butchie Boo   subB 1986.

It was such a pleasure having you as
a pupil. You are one of the lucky few,
being able to do everything with success.
I shall always follow your progress, as I
am willing to predict a bright future for
you. Have a merry Xmas and a happy time
during the summer holidays. And thank
you so much for the booties, the expensive
soap, which will go with to the hospital
and Mum's suckers at the party. I'll
miss you. All my love. Mrs L. Venter.

Opposite page (clockwise from top left): In my Natal Primary Schools colours, after making the junior Craven Week side; I have always enjoyed having pets; keeping wicket for Maritzburg College against Maritzburg East (the guy facing is none other than England batsman Kevin Pietersen); Maritzburg College on a Saturday. You can see Basher Ridge on the far side of Goldstones. I'd give anything to be back at school!

This page (clockwise from top): My De Beers team-mates and me at a soccer tournament; about to run in an athletics meet for Boland; with my Victor Ludorum trophies at Merchiston Primary; a letter I received from one of my teachers

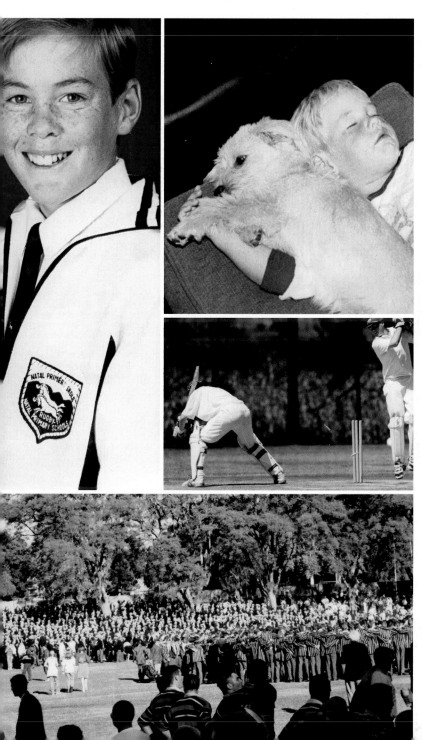

Opposite page (clockwise from top): My second Bok Test, against France at my home from home – Kings Park; getting to grips with Matt Dawson in a Test against England in 2002; dishing it out in a Sharks game against the Chiefs in 2001; more of the same against the Brumbies, also in 2001; playing for SA U21 in 2000 at No 12

This page (clockwise from top): The Maritzburg College 1st XV spent a day with the British & Irish Lions in 1997; in the thick of it for the Sharks against Western Province in the 2000 Currie Cup final; getting my backline away against Free State in the 2001 Currie Cup; My dad, Elton and me after my Test debut for the Springboks

From top: Some fans show their approval during a Test against the All Blacks; my Bok debut against France at Ellis Park in 2001

Saturdays are testing. You try your hardest to keep yourself busy but all you want is for the kick-off to arrive. At about 11am we meet in the team room, which is usually a private boardroom at the hotel that has been transformed into a meeting room. Some of the boys get strapped up – especially those with a history of knee injuries – and our team talk consists by and large of a recap of our planned moves.

We then go to our rooms to get our kitbags ready before meeting in the foyer of the hotel to leave for the game. The bus trip to the stadium is my favourite part, especially when playing in South Africa. We have a special bus bedecked in Springbok livery and as we move through the streets the supporters wave flags and shout out 'Bokke! Bokke!' The trip gets the goosebumps going and your adrenaline starts pumping nice and hard. Home-ground advantage is not just something that happens inside the stadium.

There's almost total silence – everyone is getting into the zone and you know that serious business is at hand. Most guys plug in earphones, listen to music and start to focus.

Arriving at the stadium is electric. At Kings Park you drive through the back entrance, past all the cars parked on KP1 (one of the outer fields) with people braaing, knocking back the frosties and shouting encouragement.

When the guys get out of the bus it looks like they're trying not to make eye contact and that's exactly right. At that point we just want to get away from the mayhem and into the sanctuary of our dressing room. These days a lot of effort goes into making the change room a special place for the Boks. Your name and number appear above your spot and there are inspirational posters on the walls.

We get changed into our kit, but not the jersey, just a tracksuit top to keep warm. We all try to stay as calm as possible and focus on our jobs.

No one talks when we're getting changed and considering how many of us are in the change room, the silence is quite eerie. Then it's out on to the pitch to warm up, run through a few set phases, hit some tackle bags and the kickers will take a few shots at goal. Only when we get back into the change room do we put on our match jerseys; which these days is quite a tight-fitting garment, so it's easier said than done. Next the captain (John Smit for most of my Tests) draws us into a huddle for a few words of inspiration and reminders of what we aim to do. It's all very focused, though, no head-butting or face slapping. Guys at this level don't need that. Generally, the captain will be the only one to get the revs going and reinforce what we've been talking about during the week. There are a couple of last words from the coach, a team prayer, and then you exit the change room for the anthems and the biggest game of your life – because every Test is huge.

You line up for the anthems and then it all starts flooding in. It's really emotional, but you've got to keep composed and not let it get the better of you, especially because the TV cameramen are primed to catch a tear or two! You realise you have a responsibility towards the fans and seeing the swaying masses in the stands singing the anthem and waving the South African flag never fails to move you.

On occasion I have spotted my folks and Elton singing the anthem and that really fired me up. There's no greater motivation than knowing you have family and friends right there pulling for you, just a couple of metres away. I was always very aware of their presence.

And as the strains of the national anthem die down, the moment you've dreamed of, trained for, is suddenly there and there's no time for any more contemplation.

In my earlier Tests all I wanted to do was get stuck in and put in big tackles, but as I matured and grew as a player I came to realise that as a flyhalf you are there to do a specific job and I became more focused on calling the right moves at the right time and dictating the run of play.

Leading up to the World Cup in 2007 and during the tournament I put in a lot of effort to remain calm and cool rather than get too heated. It's funny, but I have a sense of how I'm going to play when I wake up on a Saturday morning. It's very difficult to keep yourself up there and ultra keen every second of every day for 10 years, but some days I can tell are going to be better. You're bound to have off days I suppose, but that's when you have to dig deep and it becomes a test of character.

When I wake up feeling good about a game I invariably end up being in the right place, doing the right things and being in control of the flow of the game – the things a Test flyhalf is meant to do.

But enough of all the reflection. In late 2002 I had finished my eight-week suspension and had recovered from the knee op that had put me out of action after having played just six Tests for the Boks.

The operation was really painful, but Dr Ferguson was happy with my rehabilitation and efforts to get match-fit again. It had really hampered my progress and I didn't get to play for the Sharks or the Boks for most of 2002, but when I did come back I was pleased with the way I slotted back into the swing of things. It gave me good mental energy and confidence in the ability of the knee to stand up to the rigours of rugby and to know that I had taken the recovery head on, worked hard, and won through.

By now Rudolf Straeuli had been made Springbok coach and because he knew me from the Sharks and liked what I could bring to his game plan he drafted me back into the national side for the end-of-year tour to France, Scotland and England.

I was a reserve for the Test against France at the Stade Vélodrome in Marseilles and we took a good beating, 10-30. The boys were unhappy, as were the coaching staff, but we were going through a building phase for the 2003 World Cup that was looming the following year and although there were a couple of old buck in the herd, the right combinations had not yet been established so there was a lot of shifting around in terms of positions and combinations.

I started in the No 10 jersey for the next Test against Scotland at Murrayfield. I managed to slot two penalties but it was not nearly enough and we were beaten 6-21 – prompting the press to trumpet that we had suffered back-to-back record defeats.

For the final Test match of the tour, against England at Twickenham, I was switched to centre among some other changes. I was quite looking forward to partnering Fleckie (Robbie Fleck) in the midfield. He was a good mate of mine and I enjoyed the way he played, but we had not been selected alongside each other often. I was excited for the game, but that being said, there was an unsettled feel about the team and none of us saw the train coming! We were trounced by a good England side that went on to win the World Cup the following year. It was a harsh wake-up call for the players and staff alike. The South African public doesn't take it lightly when the Boks go down, even by a point, so you can imagine the outcry when we were massacred 3-53.

Our lock Jannes Labuschagne was red-carded by referee Paddy O'Brien quite early on for making contact with Jonny Wilkinson after he had kicked the ball. It was a harsh decision and it unsettled us quite a bit. I'm not saying we wouldn't have lost or that he cost us the game but losing a tight forward so early put us on the back foot and we never recovered. Nevertheless, full credit to England. They were a good side with some top-class players in their set-up – guys like their captain Martin Johnson, Lawrence Dallaglio, Neil Back, Will Greenwood and, last but not least, a great halfback combination in Matt Dawson and Jonny.

We really copped it from the public and the media and it was good to go into hiding with family and friends over

Christmas to start preparing for what was going to be an intense 2003. In the southern hemisphere the fixture list is always jam-packed, what with Super Rugby, incoming tours, outgoing tours and the Currie Cup, but 2003 was a World Cup year.

Having not been in the frame for the '99 World Cup, I was desperate to be included in the squad for Australia. I had fully recovered from the knee op and was feeling quite good but felt I wasn't quite at my best – my performances were OK but not great. The lead-up to the selection of the World Cup squad was pressurised but with the flyhalf berth wide open I quite fancied my chances. Rudolf was still in charge of the Springboks and having come through under him at the Sharks and toured with him the year before I felt we had a good understanding.

It thus came as a devastating shock when he didn't select me. Getting to the World Cup had been my major goal while recovering from knee surgery. It was hard going but every time I felt I was flagging I would remind myself, 'Butch – there's a World Cup next year, you just have to keep going'. I drove myself to get to the World Cup so it really hurt when I was left out.

I didn't expect any special treatment and didn't expect to walk into a Bok team, ever. The competition to get that green and gold jersey is really tight, but I got the feeling that Rudolf had been swayed by some of the people who were whispering in his ear. I always suspected it might have been Tim Lane, the Australian backline coach brought in by Harry, who didn't seem to have too much time for me, but who knows?

It was weird. Rudolf selected me for the Sharks and the Springboks and I know that he rated me, but when it came to the crunch he listened to the people around him rather than going with his own convictions – he turned his back on me. Rudolf's true colours would be revealed a few years down the line when he really disappointed me, but more on that later.

Louis Koen and Derick Hougaard were picked as the flyhalves instead of me and I have to admit I found it quite hard to deal with. You try to tell yourself to get on with it but you keep asking yourself 'why'? Why was I left out? Did I do something wrong? Was I just not good enough?

It was a time of much soul searching but as a wise man once said: life is lived forwards but understood backwards. So true, because as it turned out, the Springboks went on to put up a very disappointing performance at the World Cup, getting knocked out in the quarter-finals. And worst of all, when they returned, the 'Kamp Staaldraad' fiasco surfaced. With hindsight, I am really glad that I didn't have any part in any of that, but I only came to that conclusion after a few months had passed and the World Cup was over.

So it was a time for licking wounds, and you know what they say about a wounded animal – it comes back extra mad and with a lot more fire burning in its belly!

The setback was terribly disappointing, but in life we never really know what's around the corner, so I decided the best way to get over all of this was to take a break, socialise with my mates away from rugby, let my hair down, hang out like a regular guy … and what happened? I ended up meeting the woman of my dreams, whom I'd later marry.

I was out one night in Durban at a place called Pop Art and spotted a stunning blonde girl who was doing promotional work. She seemed to give off such awesome energy and I wanted to see more of her. It's true to say I was immediately bowled over, so I made sure I found out her name and where she came from.

That was during the December holidays (I think? I better be careful here because I'll get rapped over the knuckles if I get these dates wrong. I'll have to blame it on all the brain damage I've suffered from playing rugby). A bunch of mates went to St Francis Bay for New Year's and lo and behold, there was the blonde beauty I had spotted earlier in December! We started chatting and the rest, as they say, is history. Her name is Julia Westbrook. She stole my heart and took it with her to Australia (funny that) the following year as she had already made plans to travel.

Staying in contact was easier said than done but when Julia returned to South Africa in July our relationship deepened. We spent a lot of time together and as luck would have it, when she returned to Australia I was able to go too as I had a function to attend over there. I was like a bear with a sore head when I returned and didn't cope too well with the long distance thing, but thankfully after six months Julia decided to move back to Durban.

She's been with me ever since then, through all the ups and downs; I've dragged her with me to all corners of the world. She's been an amazing pillar of strength for me, to say the least.

7

THE LIGAMENTS OF LIFE

Heading into 2004, the time had come to put the disappointment of having missed out on the previous year's Rugby World Cup in Australia behind me. Life in general was good and I reminded myself that I didn't have much to complain about. For the first time in my life I was able to buy myself things. I was independent. I had started to make a decent living and was financially more secure than I had ever been.

You could say that life started making sense. I felt like I had a calling and I was in a fortunate position to at least invest some money in property and drive a decent car. Bless my mom's old Mini – may it rest in peace.

I was now a regular fixture at the Sharks. I was the first-choice flyhalf and had played a handful of games for the Springboks. I was a professional sportsman, but besides the injury setbacks I had suffered along the way, I felt very fortunate that I had recovered well and was able to do something I loved.

Kevin Putt had succeeded Rudolf Straeuli as the Sharks' coach and I felt I had something to prove after being left out of the World Cup squad. In fact, Kevin called me while I was on holiday to tell me the Sharks had signed Scottish and British & Irish Lions international Gregor Townsend, just to keep me on my toes. I went into that season hungrier than ever and I hit a purple patch of form at the start of it. I was in the best physical shape of my career, played in every game for the Sharks and seemed set to get back in the mix with the Boks.

Rudolf had been replaced by Jake White as Springbok coach following what was seen as a failed 2003 World Cup campaign as well as the outcry after details of the infamous Kamp Staaldraad (a torrid military-style survival camp the team had been subjected to) came to light.

With Jake in charge I knew that all I had to do was show good form and the rest would take care of itself. It would be an understatement to say I was really pleased with my progress during the season and knew that if I kept playing as well as I was I'd have a good chance of getting back to wearing the Bok No 10 jersey. That's all I wanted. I was dead set on getting my position back and felt confident I would be recalled.

And then disaster struck! Twelve minutes into our game against the Stormers I did my cruciate ligament. Again. And to make matters worse it was our last pool game of the tournament. But it was not a recurrence of the problem I'd had with my right knee. This time it was the left knee that had buckled. It put an immediate end to my season and put me out of rugby again for six months. I couldn't believe it. I had just come back from injury and was starting to feel so comfortable again.

The medical staff at the Sharks, Craig Roberts and Jimmy Wright, said the knee needed some serious attention. So it was back to Dr Mark Ferguson in Johannesburg. I had always had problems with my right knee – the one that had been operated on when I was 16 and again two years prior to this injury – so the fact that this had happened to my left knee was most distressing. One screwed-up knee is bad enough, let alone two!

The only recourse was more surgery. It turned out that I had torn my left ACL so it was back into theatre to have it reconstructed. One upshot was that I could speak of knee injuries as though I was a surgeon. This time there was an even larger area of damage to my articular cartilage, on the end of my femur, as well as a torn meniscus. Dr Ferguson had to perform a bone cartilage transplant and repair the meniscus. The path to recovery was one I had trodden before but my return to sport was hindered because the knee was giving further problems. I had to have another arthroscopy, which showed that the transplanted area of the cartilage had healed well. However, the damage behind my knee cap had got considerably worse. There was not much that could be done, except for a minor clean out.

There was nothing else to do but diligently go through the by now familiar rehabilitation process of physio and strengthening exercises. Under Jimmy's caring and watchful eyes, that would be my lot for the next seven months.

I make it sound glib but there was many a time I felt like throwing in the towel. As it turned out, I didn't return to action until the following year, 2005, and I've always been grateful for the part of my make-up that has helped me to fight on when it seemed there was no hope. I'd like any young schoolboy reading this, or anyone facing hardships through sport, or even life, to learn one lesson from these pages: never give up, stay true to your dreams and persevere. I know it sounds clichéd, but by now I had been written off enough times to end most careers, let alone a sporting one. I had people tell me, 'Butch, you can't carry on like this' and 'Butch, surely you're going to stop now and throw the towel in,' but I had a lot of determination and a desire to reach certain goals I had set myself. I really loved playing rugby for a living and I could not even comprehend life without it.

It doesn't matter if people tell you that you're not the best, it doesn't matter if you play for the 2nd XV at school, it doesn't matter if people tell you that you can't do it. Keep true to yourself, work hard at it and draw from the people who are close to you, the ones who give you support when the chips are down. If you succeed, the taste will be so much sweeter and if you fail, then at least you know you really did give it your best shot.

The silver lining to all of this was that it gave me a chance to get a bit of balance back into my life. As a professional I had played close on six years of solid rugby. I had focused so much energy and put so much of myself into rugby that I thought this would be a good opportunity to get back in touch with a little bit of normality; do the things that young guys do. I enjoyed a couple nights out with the boys and, despite the odd morning-after headache, kept strictly to my rehab programme.

I'm afraid to say I also got up to some mischief and one incident that immediately springs to mind is the 'bus stealing' episode which leaked to the press. Luckily that's the only one that got into the news, otherwise the public might have thought I'd lost my marbles and turned into a full-blown car thief because, truth be told, the bus was not the only vehicle I stole during this time!

Stealing a bus? This is what happened. A whole lot of us, AJ Venter included, had gone down to the South Coast for John Smit's 'bulls' (bachelors party). Smitty had a beach cottage near Pennington. We braaied, got stuck in to a few drinks and then decided to hit Margate.

We were all having a good time but the alarm bells started ringing when I noticed one of my mischievous mates in the group was missing.

And when a guy like that goes missing or is very quiet, you know that something's up. I went to look for him and eventually found him with a girl, 'making out' as the Americans would say. There was some sort of university tour going on and the group's bus was parked outside the club. I can't remember how we ended up getting into the bus – they were probably looking for a little privacy – and I ended up in the driver's seat. The bus was parked on a steep hill so when I put my foot on the clutch it would roll forward; then I'd slam the brakes so he and the girl would go flying off the back seat. I found it extremely funny; I'd apologise, and as soon as they started kissing again I'd let the bus roll down the hill and slam the brakes.

Next thing I popped the clutch out and the engine started. Well, that's all the encouragement I needed. Time for the grand tour with 'Butchie' at the wheel, but at the bottom of the hill, as I started to take the corner, I noticed the bloke in charge of the vehicle running after us, shouting and screaming. I immediately hit the brakes, pulled up the hand brake, jumped out and hid in the bushes. Luckily my mate, who was still in the bus, told the security blokes he didn't know me and that I had run down the road and around the corner; sending my pursuers in the wrong direction.

However, I got a nasty surprise the next morning when I woke up with a severe headache only to be told that the story of my escapade was already in the papers. If it had been someone else it would not even have raised a stir but in South Africa a Bok rugby player misbehaving equals big news. It goes with the territory

On another occasion we were in Cape Town and went out to Billy the Bums. I was out with Brad McLeod-Henderson and a few other blokes. We were pretty sauced up and as we were walking up the stairs, a taxi driver asked us if we needed a cab. We said no but I realised I did in fact want to call it a night. I saw the keys in the cab's ignition, jumped in, fired up the engine and took off! I did a U-turn at the next traffic lights and got a shock when I saw the police on the side of the road. What to do? My solution was to turn the car around and make my way back to our hotel in what, strictly speaking, was a stolen cab. I parked the car, left the keys in the ignition and made a beeline for my room. Luckily I heard no more as I don't think the police would have taken any excuses from me. I would have had more than a bit of explaining to do if I had been nabbed. Imagine missing out on the rest of my career for stealing cars?

One of the great characters I came to know, and who became a good mate of mine, was then Springbok and Natal Sharks prop Deon Carstens – a good guy to have on tour because there's never a dull moment with him around.

One festive season we were in St Francis on the Eastern Cape coastline. The place gets quite busy over the New Year's period and, needless to say, we had a few drinks while braaing and then ended up going out to the local club – which was packed. There are always bouncers checking IDs to keep underage youngsters away from the grog, and Deon, whose size helped him to fit the part, decided that he would make out as if he was one of the bouncers. Next thing he confronts a youngish-looking guy and demands to see his ID. The bloke produces his temporary driver's licence and what does Deon do? – he pops it in his mouth, chews it up and swallows it! Well, the guy, who was in fact over the age limit, was obviously quite upset about the whole thing and wanted to call the cops. Deon had to do some quick talking and managed to defuse the situation by handing over enough cash to pay for a new temporary licence and about 100 cane and Cokes for the guy and his mates. It led to a great quip the next day when we told the rest of our mates. They wanted to know what the poor guy looked like and someone dryly remarked: 'You can have a look when Deon goes for a shit.'

I shudder at the thought of some of the things I got up to and admit that I was stupid and irresponsible. I certainly wouldn't get up to some of those tricks now. All I can say is that we were in our 20s, living the best kind of life, and as my mom would say, boys will be boys.

Nevertheless, I go cold at the thought of some of my lucky escapes. I once ended up rolling my sponsored car. I'd had one too many and had a few cowboys as passengers in the car with me. I came off the bottom of Umgeni Road in Durban and was heading up to Billy the Bums, but tried to do a handbrake turn and flipped the car. Not far from us there was a guy having some, um, how can I best put this … action, with his girl outside her house. Luckily the car rolled and landed on its wheels and these two stopped whatever it was they were doing and came running to help us, with the bloke still pulling up his zip. I had been drinking and didn't want to get caught by the cops so this bloke suggested we quickly drive the car into his girlfriend's driveway. The lot of us sobered up pretty quickly, which I suppose tends to happen when you roll a car. I got a lift home with some other friends while a few of the others hung around to keep an eye on the car.

I returned the next morning to fetch the car and got a bit of a surprise. The previous night my car had contained a whole lot of Nike and Oakley sponsored kit, which had disappeared. I think the girl whose house it was might have helped herself to some brand new kit, but I suppose she did help me in a big way to keep me out of the clutches of the cops, so what's fair is fair. In the end she did lose out in the bargain, though, because as we drove off my mate told me he had made out with her! We high-fived and I drove the car on to the highway and headed north to get home. The funny thing was that while the roof, windscreen and side were wrecked, the car still drove OK; albeit shedding bits and pieces all the way home!

A while after that incident occurred leading KwaZulu-Natal rugby journalist Mike Greenaway told me that he had been contacted by someone who wanted to sell the story, who I think might have been the lady in the escapade, but luckily for me Mike had my back and declined to follow up on the story.

Anyway, back to rugger. I had started the 2004 season playing some of the best rugby of my life and then suffered this severe injury. I suppose all of this was partly to blame for some of the shenanigans I got up to, but it helped to get it out of the system. It hurt and was mentally testing to have come back in 2004, only to suffer another injury. Looking back, I obviously just needed to let off a bit of steam.

Remember that saying, 'All good things in moderation'? Well, a little bird whispered that it was time to get my act together. The Springbok management had undergone an overhaul and if I was to be part of the mix I needed to get that left knee of mine back in shape.

It was back to the drawing board and what I did know was that I wasn't going to let two major knee ops in three seasons keep me from regaining my Sharks and Springbok jerseys. Some called it madness but for me the pull of the black and white, and green and gold, was too strong for me to back away without a fight.

I had gone through two knee ops in three seasons and had had enough doctors' appointments to last a lifetime. I'd had enough of doctors' rooms and was amped to get back, but it was difficult to get rid of that nagging fear that I might not make it.

Jake was getting the Boks back on track and for me there was nothing worse than being wrapped up in plaster, on crutches while the guys were out on the field practising and playing. Frustration is not nearly a strong enough word to describe the despair I felt, but fortunately I was surrounded by great people who gave me a lift on my road to recovery.

Jimmy Wright was one such person. If it wasn't for him I don't think I would have ever made it back.

In the end I managed only a handful of games in 2005 before the knee issues started again. Dr Ferguson did another scope on my knee and made a few interesting findings.

The recently reconstructed ligament seemed to be in good health and the previous surface cartilage blemish had closed up nicely. However, there seemed to be a new defect in a different part of my knee joint and there was nothing more the doctors could do but clean out the debris and send me back for more rehabilitation.

This was undoubtedly the worst time I'd been through; trying to block out thoughts that my career might be over while at the same time having to force myself to go through what was extremely unpleasant and painful treatment. It's your body that's hurt but the pain in your mind is worse.

Jimmy was a pillar to lean on, but there were days when I wanted to throw in the towel. My knee would swell up at any attempt to jog, let alone run or play a game of rugby. It felt like I'd reached a dead end and the medical team must have sensed my frustration because that's when Dr Roberts, Dave Becker (head Sharks physiotherapist), Jimmy and I sat down for a meeting to discuss the way forward. It was now the last roll of the dice. Well, that's what we thought at the time.

We discussed Dr Ferguson's recommendation that we look in to a 'chondrocyte' transplant. This would require a cartilage specimen to be taken from me which would be sent overseas to be cultured in a laboratory and then re-introduced into my damaged knee. Apart from being very costly, this procedure would have needed to be performed abroad and there were no guarantees of success, and it would have added at least another six months of rehab.

I was then referred to Dr Willem van der Merwe, an orthopaedic surgeon based at the Sports Science Institute in Cape Town, for another opinion. He took a look at the knee and suggested artificial 'capping' of the damaged areas by means of a liquid metal that would instantly harden when put inside the knee. This would apparently give the knee immediate functionality.

Dr Van der Merwe consulted with Dr Ferguson and they decided we should all meet in Cape Town. It was discovered that the existing ACL wasn't functional and seemed to be contributing to the deterioration of the cartilage in my knee.

It was decided that I needed a repeat ACL reconstruction using artificial material which, depending on the outcome and the rehabilitation programme, would get me back on the field sooner than if they used tendons from my own body. To me this was the obvious way to go as I knew that having missed one World Cup, there would not be another chance for me if I missed out on France 2007. That was my mindset at the time – there was no predicting that I would indeed be part of the World Cup in New Zealand in 2011.

So it was back under the scalpel. This surgery took place in August, which meant I wouldn't play rugby for the rest of 2005 and the first half of 2006. Jimmy put together a one-day-at-a-time plan of monitoring and exercise and once again the slog began. There was no particular date in place for me to play my first official game back; all we knew was that I would need to come back stronger and fitter than ever before. It meant spending about seven hours a day in the gym, on the physio table and on the cybex machine working at improving the movement of the joint.

The early stages of becoming mobile again were tough and this is where Jimmy really came through for me. We would spend early mornings on the soft fairways of Mount Edgecombe golf course – just walking. Jimmy and I had some really meaningful conversations and he helped me to find some perspective on the setbacks I had suffered.

Jimmy emphasised the positive side of my nature, pointing out how I never really complained about being too tired or too sore. He made it easier for me and made me want to get up early and get on to the golf course before the golfers arrived. I learned about compassion for others amid my own struggles and these sessions made me feel that I could be unstoppable if I focused all my energy on that. Slowly the light at the end of the tunnel grew brighter.

The Natal Rugby Union and everyone at the Sharks were extremely supportive towards me. The Sharks family always made me feel that I had their backing, which meant a lot to me at the time.

As my movement became easier and despair turned to optimism, Jimmy and the rest of the medical staff used to rib me by calling me 'Two Weeks Butch'. This is because whenever someone would ask me about my return I would reply 'about two weeks' – even though there was still about two months to go!

And finally I was back. I played my first 20 minutes of rugby for the Wildebeest in May 2006. I came through it quite well, and managed to play for the Sharks for the remainder of the year. It sounds so matter of fact but there was something miraculous about my recovery; it taught me a great deal about myself, about life and about rugby. I couldn't have done it on my own so a big thank you to everyone who played even the smallest part.

8

BUTCHIE AND THE COMEBACK

eading into 2006 I didn't care too much for my entry in the *SA Rugby Annual*. It showed that I made my Springbok debut on 16 June 2001 against France at Ellis Park, and that I had nine Springbok caps to my credit – seven at flyhalf, one in the No 12 jersey and one in the No 17 jersey as a substitute. What it also showed is just what a gaping hole had been left by the time I'd spent recuperating from my knee injuries. I had not played in a Springbok jersey since 23 November 2002, the day we had taken such a drubbing from England.

However, Jake White was now guiding the Springboks and he was a man who had a definite plan. Jake took over from Rudolf Straeuli in January 2004 with the Boks in the doldrums following a string of record defeats and what was seen as a disastrous World Cup campaign in Australia the year before. Jake instilled a new passion and I think it came down to the simple fact that the boys wanted to play for him. He backed the guys he chose and they wanted to repay him with solid performances. Jake understood that losing can be as much a habit as winning so he planned meticulously with those players and instilled the type of game plan that would get the Boks back on the winning track.

That's not to say that everything was rosy, but from what I could see from the sidelines for two years, something positive was happening. Jake had adopted a much more attacking style of rugby and you could see by the way the boys were defending that there was some real *gees* running through the team. Jake was a careful selector who knew what he wanted from a player. A big factor in his eventual success was the way he decided John Smit was going to be his captain and the way Smitty responded with his instinct to lead by example.

Jake had a great mix of young and old. He brought Os du Randt out of retirement, and Percy Montgomery, who was playing the best rugby of his career, returned from Wales. He also kept some of the players who had caught the eye under Straeuli: Victor Matfield and Bakkies Botha, who would become the most formidable lock pairing in world rugby, and a superb duo of flankers in Schalk Burger and Juan Smith. Fourie du Preez, a man with a phenomenal rugby brain, made his debut in Jake's first Test in charge, while Bryan Habana was also awarded his first cap. Centres Jean de Villiers and Jaque Fourie provided experience and stability in the backs, but there wasn't anyone who had cemented himself as a regular first-choice flyhalf.

I was friends with and had played alongside a lot of the guys under Jake in the SA U21 side, and it was good to hear and see that there was very little politics in the camp. The boys respected each other immensely and it showed in the way they played. I got back into the Sharks mix in mid-year and as it was Tri-Nations time, the Springboks had left for Down Under. They had been beaten by France at Newlands (Jake's first home defeat) and things looked pretty topsy-turvy when they were smashed 49-0 by the Wallabies in Brisbane. The main problem seemed to be that they didn't have a solid distributor of the ball at flyhalf; someone who could set the backs loose on attack.

Jake had to do something and that's when the phone call came. The selectors felt the team needed someone with experience to take over from the flyhalves on tour, Jaco van der Westhuyzen and a young Meyer Bosman.

I was surprised but delighted to be told I had to be on the next flight to join up with the Boks. I arrived in New Zealand just two days before the Test against the All Blacks. Hectic. The coaching staff told me what they expected of me and I think they knew they wouldn't get any miracles, but were happy to know that defensively I could hold my own.

Jake had picked me because he knew how hungry I was. We played the All Blacks and while we went down 17-35, there was a distinct improvement week on week. On the way home we had to play the Aussies again and we came within seconds of overturning the 49-0 debacle, managing to restore some pride by only going down 18-20. I kicked two penalties and a conversion and, defeats aside, I was extremely happy to be back in the green and gold.

Jake picked the guys he knew and had worked with, and with me there was the additional factor of knowing how much I had missed playing for the Boks. He knew I had a lot of fight in me and that my pain could be transformed into motivation to perform. We lost the next game to the All Blacks at Loftus in Pretoria quite badly, 26-45, but then showed guts by pulling one back 21-20, in our second last outing of the Tri-Nations.

This game was played at the Royal Bafokeng Sports Palace near Rustenburg, close to Sun City, which is where we had the post-match function. I was on the bench because I hadn't been playing that well and hadn't entrenched my place as first-choice flyhalf yet, so André Pretorius wore the

No 10 jersey and he won it for us with a last-minute penalty; thus ending a run of five successive defeats against the All Blacks and also terminating their run of 15 straight victories in Tests. I got on for exactly a minute and teased the boys that I should have been the Man of the Match because the Boks were always in front while I was on the field!

There was a positive mood in the camp, despite the average results posted in the Tri-Nations. We all knew what Jake was trying to achieve and the timeline he was on. It was all about the 2007 World Cup in France and Jake was not too fussed about us going down here and there while he searched for the right combinations.

Jake was under a huge amount of pressure but he never transferred it to us. It's not for me to go into some of the issues Jake had to deal with – he wrote his own book in which his turmoil was well documented – but we were in the dark with regard to the political pressure he was under, and it was better that way. The papers, especially the Afrikaans press, were full of stories about the likelihood of Jake being fired. But he went about his business as usual. Jake treated the preparation for each game exactly the same and I gained a great deal of respect for him.

He showed a huge amount of faith in me and for that I will always be grateful. However, let's get one thing straight – I would never have been kept in the flyhalf position for the Boks if I did not perform. It doesn't work like that and Jake certainly doesn't work like that. He would always give you a fair run, but if you started slipping he'd let you know that you were heading in the wrong direction, believe you me. This mutual respect meant that I wanted to shine for him.

Jake took a lot of flak for a few of his selections, but let's face it, the man was right most of the time, wasn't he? How many people called him crazy when he brought Monty back into the mix? Monty ended up playing the best rugby of his life under Jake.

A lot of people thought that Jake was losing it when he called me back into the Springbok fold, but I also knew that there were many fans who were happy to see me back and that gave me a huge amount of motivation. I wanted to step up and play as well as I could for them.

The love/hate relationship the public seemed to have with me has always struck me as being slightly strange. I'm not saying that people have been unreasonable and had it in for me, but there have always been two camps – those who were Butch James fans and those who were not.

The Sharks fans were always really supportive and I got a lot of encouragement from them but at times I was given a bit of a roasting by Springbok fans and those from other provinces. The press also used to put in their two cents' worth; some of it bad, some of it good, but it always felt nice to prove them wrong. I knew there were critics who had written me off and it motivated me to silence them.

I suppose it's part and parcel of swimming in the goldfish bowl that is professional sport. It's just the way it is and most pro sportsmen have to put up with it; some more than others, though. In my case, when I'd come back from injury, people would say, 'He'll never be the same, his best days are over'. But I can honestly say that I came back a better player after every injury I sustained.

I don't know why, but I just got better over the years despite the setbacks. Although people are entitled to their opinions, I find it strange that some have this misconception of me. Those who don't really know me may think that I'm bigheaded and *windgat* (a show off) but those who are close to me know I'm actually a shy, reserved kind of guy at heart and find a good laugh to be one of life's vital ingredients. So cheers to all those who never wrote me off – the comeback was made that much sweeter because of you!

At the end of 2006 a Springbok squad was chosen to go on the usual end-of-year tour and I was chuffed to be included.

As I mentioned earlier, we had some really special players in the mix. Jean, Schalk and I found common ground. We became good buddies and besides being really good players, they are great guys. I have often said that Schalk should have played his rugby in the old days because he does it for the sheer fun and passion of it; he plays his heart out so that he can enjoy a cold beer with the boys after the game. He's probably the player I rate most highly, because he always gives 100% no matter what.

Jaque Fourie is one of the characters of the side, a prankster if ever there was one, but an awesome rugby player too. It also felt special to have played alongside a legend like Os. I was 15 when he started playing for the Springboks, which shows just how long he anchored our scrum. Os is a really *lekker* guy. He was obviously a lot older than all of us, but remained young at heart and enjoyed a bit of fun when it was going around. Everyone in the set-up under Jake got along. There was hardly ever any animosity; we were all mates and enjoyed each other's company on and off the field. We had a real sense of camaraderie – which is an often overlooked ingredient to success.

Even though our results had been disappointing, there was a sense of purpose when the Springbok squad met to prepare for the tour to Ireland and England. I had played just a handful of games under Jake, but I sensed that the mood was right and that we were headed in the right direction. We were very keen to start clicking as a team and with a collective eye on the World Cup there was a sense of urgency as we boarded our plane for the flight north.

Our first Test was against Ireland in Dublin but I wasn't in the starting line-up. Jake wanted to try new combinations – like playing Bryan Habana at centre. He told me he wanted to play me in the first clash against the English, which I understood, but I was still quite disappointed as the Test at Lansdowne Road marked a century of the Springbok badge.

It had been arranged that the team would play in kit that replicated the strip worn by Paul Roos' 1906 side, who became the first 'Springbokken'. As it turned out, the team didn't play well and were beaten by a highly-charged Irish side. I still ended up getting that special jersey, though. You are always given two match jerseys and it was cool of Wynand Olivier to give me his spare one.

The next week we took on England at Twickenham in what turned out to be a significant game for me as I felt my performance that day pushed me to the front of the flyhalf queue. Instead of staying in London, it had been decided we would set up camp in Bath for the lead-up to the Test. We were doing some stretching exercises at a practice session in which we were required to lift an arm and a leg. Little did I suspect what it would lead to. The trainer was chirping me because I was pointing my index finger to the sky and my retort was that that was exactly what I was going to do when I scored in the match come Saturday. And that is what happened. I scored a beaut of a try, which will always be one of my most special moments in a Springbok jersey in a game that felt like my best in the green and gold.

I was rooming with Jean that week and it was he who passed me the miracle ball to the inside which I scored off. It was quite funny because we were watching some boxing on TV during the week in our hotel room and the guy who won the fight kept on saying to his coach, 'I deserve it! I deserve it!' so Jean ran up to me after I scored, shouting, 'You deserve it! You deserve it!'

I scored that try and was successful with a conversion and two penalties, but yet again the match had turned into the Battle of Wounded Knee. As early as the fifth minute I had felt my knee go but I didn't want to leave the field. I had Jake's words as we left the change room in the back of my mind: 'If you break your leg, then strap the bladdy thing to your back and carry on!' I knew my cartilage had gone but had no choice but to carry on and was pleased that I did, otherwise I would never have had the wonderful memory of scoring a superb try at Twickenham.

I was man down once again and had to return home for another op in which the doctors removed a huge piece of cartilage. To make matters worse, we ended up allowing England to get out of jail in a match we had been well in control of. Phil Vickery was shoved over near the end for a try and conversion that consigned us to a 21-23 defeat.

As they say about the English weather: it never rains but it pours. But this group of players had something bigger in the back of their minds and we knew we had just started our journey as a group. The next weekend we reversed that result against England, beating them 25-14 and ending a run of seven consecutive losses against them.

9

RUSH AND ROULETTE

Despatches from the press on my performance in the Twickenham Test against England were universally complimentary but only served to heighten my frustration at having suffered another knee injury. I really thought that the game, in which I had earned my 14th Test cap, was a turning point in my Springbok career. It was interesting to note that the reporters agreed, to the extent that many of them lambasted Jake White for having substituted me. Jake was under severe pressure and another defeat after a poor Tri-Nations did not go down well. Unaware that I was crocked, the journos felt Jake had made an unwarranted substitution that cost the Boks the Test match.

The truth came out when it emerged that I was on my way home to seek medical assistance yet again. Even though I had built up quite a lot of resilience towards this whole process of rehabilitation I was feeling very low and made up my mind that this was it; I would give it one more go and quit if the injury did not heal fully.

I agreed to go for surgery in the hope that I would recover in time to realise my dream of making the Springbok World Cup squad in 2007. But I made no bones about the fact that if my knee went one more time, I was going to call it a day. A man can only do so much and your knees can only take so much punishment. My knees had by now suffered well beyond what could be considered a normal amount of abuse. If the knee went, so would I.

Besides my goal of going to the 2007 World Cup I also felt I needed to dig deep one last time for the KwaZulu-Natal Rugby Union, which had been so good to me.

I had a scope done on my left knee and the good news was that the damage was not as severe as feared. I had to have a small part of my meniscus (cartilaginous tissue in the knee) shaved off but my ACL was in good shape so the rehab would be shorter and less intense. There was hope.

I had been injured on 18 November 2006 and was able to push myself to a point of readiness for the start of the Super 14 in 2007. It was like walking on eggshells but I managed to make my way back into the Sharks team and felt relatively strong in the games I played.

However, a rather upsetting new phenomenon began to crop up and I started to suspect someone was after me as I was 'randomly' tested for drug use three games in a row. Someone really seemed to think I had taken steroids to recover as fast as I had and wanted me cuffed for it. It isn't uncommon to get tested, but when my number was pulled three times in a row I knew something was up, but the fact that I tested negative on each occasion helped to get me over my irritation.

With former Springbok centre Dick Muir as our new coach, the Sharks were ready. Dick was an old stalwart of Natal rugby. He earned 148 caps for Natal in the early-90s and then moved to Western Province for a few seasons. He skippered Province against the British & Irish Lions and also to victory in the Currie Cup in 1997. He went on to earn five Springbok caps under Nick Mallett in the mid-90s, signing off with a 100% win record.

You got the feeling that Dick was always a Natal boy at heart. He grew up on a farm in the Natal countryside – on the Cedarville flats between Kokstad and Matatiele – and became a boarder at Queen's College in Queenstown in the Eastern Cape. He returned to Natal to study a course at Cedara College of Agriculture near Howick, before making his debut for the Natal side.

Dick was quite new to coaching but had done well in a short space of time. He got good results out of the guys because he was always one of the boys. He would drill the team during practices, get the result on the Saturday and then join the guys for a few beers after the game. His style of working and socialising with the team created a mutual bond and we wanted to play for him.

With Dick at the wheel we got the 2007 Super 14 under way. Our side had a good balance of some old heads mixed with youthfulness, and personally I was feeling good. The Sharks squad was strong, had depth, and contained some notable players in Deon Carstens, John Smit, Bismarck du Plessis, BJ Botha, AJ Venter, Ryan Kankowski, Bob Skinstad, Ruan Pienaar, Brad Barritt, JP Pietersen, Frans Steyn and Percy Montgomery.

Our first game of the tournament was against a Bulls side packed full of quality players in Victor Matfield, Fourie du Preez, Bryan Habana, Gary Botha, Danie Rossouw, Pedrie Wannenburg and Wikus van Heerden. There was a sea of blue jerseys in the stands because Bulls supporters are so passionate and *mal* (crazy) about their team that they will drive, catch a plane, a train, a bus, hitchhike or even walk to get to a Bulls fixture. We knew the opening game would be a big one, as it always is between the Bulls and the Sharks. There's no love lost, I can promise you that.

The Bulls came out firing and hammered away at us. They should have probably been rewarded but thanks to our fierce defence we were able to hold them out. After absorbing the pressure we could start playing our own game and gave the ball some air. A superb passage of play brought us our first score. Monty (Percy Montgomery) fielded a chip and chase and moved the ball to Frans; the ball then moved wide through Kanko's (Ryan Kankowski) hands, sending JP over for a try. We went into the change room at half-time with a lead of only seven points but came back out determined to maintain our tempo. It worked as the boys from up north began to wilt in the steamy Durban weather. We worked JP over for a second try and with Monty coolly slotting both conversions we sealed a 17-3 win.

We couldn't have hoped for a better start. Beating the Bulls is always special and this was the kind of victory in which it was hard to single out individuals. It was a huge team effort in which we showed guts and capitalised on our opportunities. What we didn't know then was that this would not be the last time we would be seeing the Bulls in the Shark Tank that season.

We were up and running and, more importantly, I was up and running in what would become a landmark season for the Sharks, who would become the first South African side to top the log and host a final. We had a few close calls but a run of six straight wins to start the competition put us on the right track.

Super Rugby is not for the faint-hearted, though, and we were given a wake-up call when we went down to the Brumbies at home in week seven and then took another knock when we dropped our first game on the road – to the Western Force in Perth. What made it hurt more was that this was my 50th game for the Sharks.

Our wins had come against the Bulls, the Waratahs, the Highlanders, the formidable Crusaders, the Cheetahs and the Hurricanes, but these setbacks showed what makes the Super Rugby tournament so exciting. You learn very quickly that the teams are evenly matched and that if you take your foot off the pedal even slightly, you'll be beaten. That's the beauty of the competition; on any given day any team can beat any other so you always have to be up for it. Monty was right in the groove with his goal-kicking and I was enjoying the partnership I was striking up with my inside centre, Brad Barritt. Brad put me in for the try that sealed the win against the Waratahs, which I felt was testimony to the understanding developing between us. I enjoyed playing with him as not only was he a strong runner but he also had a great sense of the right angles and I revelled in putting him away into gaps.

It was not all plain sailing, though, because while I was feeling strong I continued to deal with what had by now become a regular occurrence – my knee swelling up after every game. I needed to be treated with care, or managed as the coaches say nowadays, because I think Jake had already whispered to Dick that he wanted to take me to the World Cup later that year, provided I was fit. Dickie played his part and stood me down when he felt it was the right time.

The season was building into something good but I still had the feeling someone had it in for me. Random tests of players to check for performance-enhancing substances are commonplace but it was strange, to say the least, that I got tested regularly. It actually felt like it was every flippin' week! Every time they needed someone to provide a urine sample it seemed to be me, and it felt kind of weird. There was some history. When I was operated on previously, an appeal was made to Dr Ismail Jakoet, Saru's (South African Rugby Union) chief medical officer and a ranking official in the SA Institute for Drug Free Sport, to be allowed to insert a steroid into my knee during the procedure. Medical research showed that it wouldn't affect my performance in any way, but would accelerate my rate of recovery. However, the request was turned down and the surgery was completed without the use of any steroids. I don't know who or what was behind all of this, but it just felt like I was being tested at almost every opportunity. Someone in a high place who was not a Butch James fan seemed determined to get me snagged on suspicion that steroids had been used; hence my rapid recovery. Needless to say, I tested negative every time.

Maybe I should use this opportunity to put a few rumours to rest. I have never in my life taken anabolic steroids to enhance my performance or help me to recover from an injury. I've always worked extremely hard physically and undergone huge amounts of mental strain to claw my way back into the fold of playing for the Boks, my province or my club. That, essentially, is what this book is about. A person called Butch James. A person who's been written off a million times over, undergone numerous operations yet still found the inner strength and perseverance to work his way back into the fold by means of sheer mental guts and determination. So … have I ever used steroids? The answer is negative, always has been and always will be. I've never been a fan of guys who use steroids.

While we're at it, I might as well clear out the cupboard and put all the other rumours about me to rest, even though it saddens me to have to write about such nonsense when all I ever wanted to do was play great rugby for my union and represent the Springboks. That's all that really mattered to me; I was never one for the politics and the sideshows.

Quite apart from efforts to pin the use of performance-enhancing drugs on me, I was also accused of dabbling in narcotics or recreational drugs – in my case, according to the rumours that were spread, I was not only using cocaine but was also dealing in the white powder!

That's a serious accusation and after digging under the surface a little it turned out that one of the married guys in the Sharks set-up was getting a little worked up because his mistress was flirting with me. His jealous reaction was to spread vicious gossip that I was dealing and doing cocaine. How pathetic can you get – especially when you apply some logic to the accusation? My day consisted of a few hours of gym every morning, rehabilitation on my knee, lunch with my girlfriend Julia or some team-mates, and practice almost every afternoon or evening with games almost every Saturday. When on earth was I going to get a chance to drive around dealing in cocaine? The whole thing was so ridiculous but quite hurtful, and potentially very damaging to my career. I should also mention that there were quite a few guys' names that were pulled into these rumours, and I know the stories did their rounds, which is all very sad.

This whole business of cocaine reared its head again a few years later when I was at Bath. But more about the Bath saga later on.

So back to the rugby. Of all the South African sides, the Sharks have by far the best record overseas and we got our 2007 season back on track by thumping the Reds and then skipping 'across the pond' to New Zealand and lowering the colours of the Blues. We were riding high again and a place in the semi-finals was beckoning.

We had one more game to play on tour, against the Chiefs, and I was surprised when Dick decided to drop me from the starting line-up in favour of Frans Steyn. However, things didn't go according to plan and we went into the shed at half-time trailing 3-25. Dick decided to bring me on early in the second half and I worked hard at making a positive impact. We threatened the Chiefs' lead by scoring four tries in a sensational second half, but it was all a little too late and we went down 27-35. However, I wondered whether that second half had made an impression on Jake watching back home. The World Cup in France was drawing ever nearer and I suppose we all had that on our minds.

Back home we beat the Lions at Ellis Park to move to second place on the table, just a point shy of the Crusaders, and it dawned on us that it might be possible to top the log – thus ensuring a home semi-final and also a home final if we won through. Everything was going well and it was around this time that a couple of us would often stop off at a casino after a few post-match beers.

I'm quite keen on the odd flutter and, as with the Sharks, the numbers were falling for me. One night a session on the tables netted me R20 000, which I bragged about to Julia and some of our close mates when I got home. Next morning I woke with a sore head, went for a run to clear the cobwebs, and forgot about the windfall of the night before.

The week rolled into its usual routine of practices, gym and time with the medics and when we won again on the Saturday my thoughts again turned to giving the old roulette wheel a whirl. I was feeling upbeat but luck was against me this time. I blew about R3 000 but then remembered the R20 000 I had won the week before and stupidly stashed in the cubbyhole of my car. So I ran out into the parking lot, took R2 000 out and ran back into the casino to make up what I had lost. Well, I lost that R2 000 in no time! So … I ran back to the car and fetched another wad, only to lose it even faster than the previous two grand. I was now hitting that point of no return but, being the strong-headed individual that I am, I decided to go back to the car again and fetch another R2 000, and lost that too! This carried on until I had almost lost the whole lot and came up with the bright idea that my luck might change if I moved from the Sun Coast Casino to Sibaya Casino out on the north coast. I had frittered away nearly R20 000 but the logic that is enhanced by a few cane and Cokes convinced me that a change of scenery might do the trick.

I walked into Sibaya at about 2am with empty pockets and had to draw more money. I suppose I should have cut my losses but I was determined to win back what I had lost. So I went to the tables and, like my injuries, things slowly got better. Time seemed to fly by and when I noticed it was 5am I decided to cash in my chips. I walked out the front doors of the Sibaya Casino with R50 000, in R200 notes, stuffed into my pants! The wind blew some of the notes away so there was Butch James, Springbok flyhalf, tackling R200 notes in a car park at 5am in the morning. Might have made a juicy piece for the press if that had got out.

Our final match of the round-robin stage was against the Stormers in Cape Town. We were really amped to beat the 'mountain goats' to clinch our place in the semis. AJ Venter epitomised our attitude. AJ, a stalwart and regular in our starting line-up, had suffered a broken index finger in the game against the Lions but he insisted on playing and his presence was a huge factor.

Newlands is always full but for this game it was literally packed to the rafters. The Stormers were no slouches with names like Schalk Burger, Luke Watson, Joe van Niekerk, Breyton Paulse and De Wet Barry in the side. We took early control of the game in all respects but, most importantly, on the scoreboard with two rapid-fire tries, going to the break with a 21-10 lead. In the second half we adopted a more defensive approach; our forwards did an amazing job in the set pieces and rucks and mauls to keep the Stormers on the back foot. With a guy like Schalk in their midst the Stormers can be a relentless side and they certainly gave it their all, but it wasn't enough. We ended up winning the game 36-10. It was one of the most satisfying victories in all my time with the Sharks and it became even better when we realised we had topped the log because the Crusaders had suffered an almost unprecedented loss at home to the Chiefs in their final game.

We had won, we were guaranteed a semi-final at Kings Park and our game against the Stormers turned out to be the prelude to arguably the most remarkable Super Rugby performance ever by a South African side. The Bulls had seemed out of it but had made a strong run from the back of the field. They needed a 44-point victory over a Reds team coached by Eddie Jones to overtake the Blues into third place and a 72-point win to overhaul the Crusaders to take second spot. We were well into our celebratory party and every now and then someone would call out another score as the Bulls amassed an amazing 92-3 victory.

That meant two South African teams had finished first and second and our semi-final was to be against the Blues, with the shattered Crusaders having to rapidly change their plans to fly to Pretoria to take on the Bulls.

The build-up to that semi-final was almost of Test match proportions. We were very determined to be the first South African side to host a Super Rugby final and worked hard during the week. The Blues came out firing and held on to the ball in the first quarter, but failed to convert pressure into points. For our part we tackled like Trojans, survived a few heart-stopping moments against a Blues team that had brought its A game and kept our line intact.

We took a 9-3 lead as the game rolled in to the second quarter and we started to dominate. It wasn't long before Kanko did some outstanding work to set up hardworking Johann Muller for the first try of the game and his first in Super Rugby. The Blues earned a penalty on the stroke of half-time to add three points, which meant we went into the break 14-6 up.

It threatened to go pear-shaped at the start of the second period as the Blues scored two tries, one of which was converted, to wrest the lead. The Blues, like all New Zealand sides, are exceptionally dangerous when their tails are up, but they were not about to spoil our fairytale. Composure wins big games and Monty steadied the ship by slotting some crucial kicks, giving us the lead going into the final

20 minutes. We built up some phases and I decided to start spreading the ball, running the Kiwis from left to right and gradually the gaps started to open up. I darted through one of these holes for what turned out to be the try that sealed our win. It was a massive performance and John Smit dedicated the win to the crowd. 'Things kept turning around, we played against a class act and the game could have gone either way. But with a crowd like this, it wasn't going to be difficult.'

The game was ours, 34-18, and 51 233 rampant Sharks fans streamed out to the B-field for what was surely the best party anywhere in the oval world. Our own celebration was muted because we were already focusing on playing the Bulls, who had hammered the Saders 27-12 in their semi-final. Little did we know what heartbreak was to follow or, on the other hand, what an excellent advertisement it was for two South African sides to have been in the Super 14 final a few months away from France's World Cup.

The build-up to the final was huge. We felt the force of every single Natalian behind us and tickets were sold out in a matter of minutes. The Bulls had a very good side, but we'd beaten them in the opening game of the season on our home turf and we knew we could do it again.

On the morning of the final I woke up feeling good about what lay ahead; ready to perform for the 54 000 spectators who were expected to sardine into the Kings Park precinct for the game. I had played a solid season, my knee had stood up and there was a maturity to my game that might have been lacking previously. I felt I was controlling games as I was expected to do.

Conditions on that Saturday were perfect. The nerves were working good and proper and the alert button was on as we ran out. This Sharks team had a great deal of determination, courage and commitment and we started with one thing in mind, and that was to win. The Bulls were on the receiving end of some physical bullying as we contested every phase, breakdown and aspect of play with the kind of physicality the Bulls were renowned for.

But it was the Bulls who drew first blood when Pierre Spies scored a soft try off a movement from a lineout. There had been a slip-up in our defensive pattern and Smitty gave us a good talking to behind the poles. It was one of those moments when the game could have slipped away but we lifted our heads and immediately hit back with a try from JP. We were forcing the Bulls to make twice as many tackles as ourselves and went into half-time 14-10 up.

Dickie and Smitty pumped us up and sent us back out firing. Again it was the Bulls who scored first with a penalty that pulled them to within a point of us, setting up a fight to the death. We had the upper hand in the physical exchanges and denied the Bulls the chance to set a solid platform and attack off the front foot. They also battled to come to terms with our tactical game and between Monty, Frans and me we decided to alternate between tight, close-quarter stuff, a kicking game and quick, attacking play, which kept them guessing throughout.

We hammered away at each other, the game swung from end to end and with just two minutes left on the clock it seemed the gods were smiling on us as we were awarded a penalty. With Smitty having been subbed we bravely decided to kick for touch to set up an attacking lineout. We won the lineout and settled into our tight hit-up formation, pick and go, pick and go and then suddenly Albert van den Berg found a hole and was shoved over. The Sharks fans went into an absolute frenzy and the scoreboard showed: Sharks 19 Bulls 13. It flickered through my mind that a successful conversion would put us eight points up and make it impossible for the Bulls to overhaul us in the time that was left.

But what followed was like a sequence from a bad dream. Monty had been taken off, I'm not sure why, but we still had a good kicker in Ruan Pienaar and I was also up to take the kick. It was not a difficult conversion attempt – just inside where the 15m and 22m lines cross to the right of the poles – and was the kind of kick you'd expect to get. I called for the ball; with Monty off the field I was the most experienced kicker and felt confident of slotting it. But Frans already had the ball and was adamant he was going to take the kick, so I stood back. If a guy shows that sort of confidence, then let him go for it. He seemed pretty sure of himself so I backed him. His body language was such that I felt he was going to knock it through. Frans took the ball and the rest of us retreated to the halfway line with literally a minute left on the clock. One thing none of us senior players did, though, was to tell Frans to take his time and chew into the remaining minute on the clock. I think we took it for granted. But to our dismay he placed the ball quickly, rushed his kick, and pulled it!

The fact that we lost wasn't Frans' fault, because there are 15 guys on the field and there was another huge blunder to follow anyway. You have to deal with cruel realities when you are a kicker. Get them over and you are a hero, miss and you are the villain. Frans would have gotten that kick over nine times out of 10.

But what followed proved to be fatal. The Bulls kicked off with probably one movement left in the game. Their only hope was to try to regain possession, keep the ball alive and try to score a converted try. Victor Matfield accomplished the first task by getting the ball back and the Bulls started to string the phases together, creeping deeper into our territory. One mistake by them and it was over, but in a passage of play in which the ball went to ground, referee Steve Walsh not only missed the fact that a Bulls player on the other side of the ruck was playing the ball on the ground, but also knocked it forward. That should have been the game right there, but Walsh missed it and allowed play to continue. The ball came out, Bryan Habana cut in from the right, broke inside, found a hole, straightened and went over next to the poles. That was that; a kicker of Derick Hougaard's calibre was never going to miss a conversion as simple as that one.

Bulls 20, Sharks 19. I'll never forget the stunned silence that settled on Kings Park. I was told later that some fans had been celebrating so furiously that they were not even aware that Bryan had scored and nicked the game from us.

It was meant to be the crowning glory of a great season, but was stolen from us in the cruelest manner imaginable. There was a lot of discussion and unhappiness about Walsh missing the fact that the ball was played illegally on the ground and that there was a knock-on at the last ruck. But be that as it may, we lost and should have killed the game by then. We should have dealt better with the ball in those closing moments. That's sport for you. You can climb high mountains but you can also sink into the deepest seas. It's what keeps us addicted. As Andy Colquhoun wrote in the 2008 *SA Rugby Annual*: 'No team will ever get closer to winning the Super Rugby competition than the Sharks, who had the title snatched from their hands two minutes after the siren had sounded on the season's end. It was a bitter, bitter way for a memorable campaign to end – all the more because they were the architects of their own downfall.'

It was a huge blow mentally. The boys were gutted as we dragged ourselves back into the change room. I don't even want to go on about it because even thinking about it makes me mad. I would wake up in the middle of the night for the next few weeks that followed and think about how we lost that game. But from that haunted, painful feeling some good would come. I carried that experience into the World Cup final in Paris a few months later and swore that I would never experience something like that ever again.

10

WORLD CHAMPIONS, NO PROBLEM

Modern-day rugby being as intense as it is, I had no time to get over Bryan Habana nabbing the Super 14 title away from us – the show had to go on. My focus quickly switched to the next engagement, which would take place the following week – the Boks vs England in the first of two Tests.

The squad contained many Sharks and Bulls players and within a day of climbing into each other during the Super 14 final, we were back together in the Bok camp, having to be buddies again. We were hurting but I was impressed with the way Victor Matfield and his boys handled the situation. There was no gloating and rubbing it in; just a switch of focus to what lay ahead of us – the Rugby World Cup in France in September and October.

We had started on the road towards winning the World Cup years before, but there was a real shift in focus in what was a good year for us in 2007. England were going to be in our World Cup pool in France and in these two home Tests we struck a major psychological blow by thrashing their, albeit understrength, side 58-10 in Bloemfontein and then 55-22 in Pretoria a week later.

In the second Test the English did shock us by taking a 17-19 lead at half-time, but Jake gave us a sharp talking-to and we upped our intensity, scoring 33 points in the last 30 minutes of the game to claim an aggregate 113-32 victory in the series. They made much of the fact that they had been forced to tour with a side stripped of many frontline players but these two wins, allied to a Test victory scored on tour the year before, meant that, crucially, we had gained the mental upper hand.

Next up was the Tri-Nations and we snatched a dramatic victory over Australia at Newlands that must have left them feeling a bit shattered. They started the game with a lot of intent and were up for the challenge. However, we enjoyed a lot of possession and scored a good try in the 13th minute after the ball had gone through four phases. I picked up a pass off my toes and sent Jaque Fourie over. We had played OK but found ourselves on the wrong side of the scoreboard with just a few minutes left, but that's when Frans Steyn showed what a special player he is by coolly slotting two long-range drop goals to take us home, 22-19.

Next it was the All Blacks in Durban. I was very pumped up for this game as it was our last big Test before the World Cup, it was my home ground and I've always loved playing at Kings Park.

The game had the usual characteristics of an All Blacks-Springboks Test – extremely physical and tough. We went into half-time with an 11-6 lead after Schalk Burger scored just before the break. We knew we had them on the ropes and came out firing. The ball came out on the All Blacks' side and Rodney So'oialo tried to pop the ball up from a tackle, but I read it and collected the ball for a breakaway try, which put us up 18-9.

I always joke with my mates that that was the day I outran Joe Rokocoko – but it's hardly true because Rokocoko was probably the fastest rugby player on the planet at the time and I wasn't exactly the quickest guy around; the way the ball fell meant I had a big start on him.

I tweaked my hamstring while scoring the try and had to come off. Frans came on to replace me at a time when we were under a bit of pressure. The first thing he had to do was make a clearance kick to get us out of trouble. Things went a bit wrong, and the All Blacks got a 5m scrum which they scored from; that's when they got their tails up. We fell asleep a bit and were running bad lines when chasing up the kicks. The game spiralled out of control and we ended up losing 21-26. It was a cruel match to watch unfold, but that's Test rugby for you. However, what this game did show was that if there was a team out there that could unsettle the All Blacks, it was us.

After the match Jake told us that those players who would definitely be going to the World Cup wouldn't be travelling to Australia and New Zealand for the away leg of the Tri-Nations, but would be sent for two weeks of conditioning and fitness work in Cape Town.

It was a good call. Jake's plan was that while we were getting a necessary spell of rest, the other guys would go over and fight for their places in the World Cup squad. The boys didn't play at all badly on the away leg. They actually started off very well against Australia in Sydney, only to squander their 17-0 lead to go down 17-25. Against the All Blacks at the Jade Stadium in Christchurch the following week Johann Muller had the distinction of becoming South Africa's 53rd Springbok captain after Bob Skinstad had been forced to return home from Australia due to a rib injury. Again the side gave a good account of itself; the All Blacks were flattered by the 6-33 scoreline. With 11 minutes to go the score was 6-12 – the Boks being undone by three quick-fire tries after Pedrie Wannenburg had been somewhat unfairly yellow-carded by Stuart Dickinson.

In the meantime, the rest of us were sent to Cape Town where we were knocked into shape by Rassie Erasmus. That's when former Wallabies and Brumbies coach Eddie Jones came into the mix. We did a lot of fitness stuff, getting our bodies into shape and clear of injuries. But any thoughts of it being an uneventful time were blown away by an incident between Percy Montgomery and me.

The Bok management had good vision and saw merit in sending us for a few French lessons. The thinking was that it would stand us in good stead during the World Cup and would help to win over a bit of support from the French public if we could string together a bit of their language.

During one of these lessons I was sitting between Monty and Jean de Villiers. The teacher was making us repeat a few sentences, which is when Jean and I started mocking Monty in French. We were laughing and Monty started getting worked up. We were saying things like, 'Aah, Montee can hardly speak Engleesh, how can you expect him to say anything in French?' Monty then asked the teacher what we were saying and she told him we weren't being very nice.

So we carried on, taking it a step too far. Monty lost it and swung a punch at me in anger; it connected with my shoulder. It didn't bother me, but there was an Afrikaans TV crew busy filming and suddenly they were getting a scoop – the Springboks getting into a punch-up while preparing for the World Cup. It wasn't ideal but I was more embarrassed than anything else; I didn't want that sort of thing leaking to the media. I mean, imagine if that footage had landed up on the news that night for the whole country to see?

Luckily we were a tightly knit bunch of guys so we sorted it out pretty quickly. I left it and noticed Monty was very encouraging towards me the next day at practice. That was our last day in Cape Town and afterwards I went back to my hotel room, took a shower and started packing my bag because we were leaving to go home. I heard a knock at the door and it was Monty. He had come to apologise. He had tears in his eyes and said he was extremely sorry. He said he had just cracked and didn't mean it. I was cool with it. So we shook hands and left it at that. Monty and I are good mates to this day. The whole thing was nothing really, but it could have become nasty if the media had run with it.

We then played Namibia at Newlands in a warm-up game and posted a score of 105-13. This was the second-biggest score the Boks had ever recorded and the third time the Boks had run up a ton of points. It was obviously a weak Namibia team, but it gave us an opportunity to put some things into practice and allowed Monty to sign off in style in what was supposed to be his last Test match on South African soil. Monty and Os du Randt were given the honour of leading the team out; they both scored tries and Monty contributed a record 35 points. Heading for the World Cup it was good to know we had a kicker of his calibre in our midst.

The countdown was in full swing and we played in two more warm-up games to add the finishing touches to our preparation. We headed over to Ireland where we were given a good battle by club side Connacht before winning 18-3. Then it was across the Irish Sea to play Scotland at Murrayfield. The media reviews of our 27-3 victory were unflattering but Jake was pretty happy with how we had played. Our defence was solid and Jake was satisfied that we had perfected a style of play that would be successful in France. We were ready for the World Cup and raring to go.

The squad for the World Cup that had been named on 21 June was positively received; the headline on SuperSport's website summed up the general feeling: 'Jake gets his Dream Team'. The 30-man squad looked like this ...

Backs: Jean de Villiers, Fourie du Preez, Jaque Fourie, Bryan Habana, Butch James, Ricky Januarie, Percy Montgomery, Akona Ndungane, Wynand Olivier, Ruan Pienaar, JP Pietersen, André Pretorius, Frans Steyn, Ashwin Willemse.

Forwards: Bakkies Botha, BJ Botha, Gary Botha, Schalk Burger, Os du Randt, Victor Matfield, Johann Muller, Danie Rossouw, Bob Skinstad, John Smit (captain), Juan Smith, Pierre Spies, Gurthrö Steenkamp, Albert van den Berg, CJ van der Linde, Wikus van Heerden.

Unfortunately Pierre was forced to drop out of the squad after the discovery of blood clots in his lungs. The selectors took the significant decision to replace him with the young Sharks hooker Bismarck du Plessis.

There was a quiet confidence within the squad as we made our way to France. Our preparation could not have been better and we found ourselves in the almost unheard of situation in the modern game of carrying no injuries within the squad. The final touch came from an unexpected quarter. Nelson Mandela was in Paris and we were invited to meet with him at his hotel. He delivered a few words of inspiration. He need not have said anything – it was just so awesome to be in his presence; he really was and will always be a very inspirational person.

Our first game was against Samoa at the Parc des Princes in Paris on Sunday, 9 September. We ran in eight tries to win 59-7, but that does not begin to tell the story of a highly-charged occasion. There were some heavy hits flying about as per usual when playing Samoa, and we were rocked by the disciplinary issues that ensued. Schalk clashed with scrumhalf Junior Polu as they both jumped for the ball, and was cited; belatedly I must add. We were also worried that Juan Smith might be cited for throwing a punch but in the end the full weight of the disciplinary process came down on Schalk. We were outraged when he was suspended for four matches (later reduced to two on appeal).

There was definitely a feeling that they were out to get us but in the end the whole incident probably stiffened our resolve. In the end the game will be remembered for Bryan's four tries – emulating former Bok wing Chester Williams' performance against Samoa in the 1995 World Cup. We were playing England the next week and were happy with our opening statement against Samoa. There was one final disappointing twist to this game, however, when we learned that Jean had picked up a bicep injury, which meant the end of his World Cup. I really felt for Jean; this was the second time he would miss out on a World Cup due to injury.

We took on England at the Stade de France the next week and seldom has a stadium announcement sounded as good as it did that night after that game: 'Souss Africa, Sirty seex, Eengland neel!' We gave an immense performance that night in the French capital to stack up a 36-0 victory over England. We were very focused and clinical in our execution. I felt settled and was happy with the way I controlled the game – made easier by the fact that Fourie du Preez proved he was the best scrumhalf in world rugby that day.

Our next game was against Tonga at the Stade Félix Bollaert in Lens. The Tongans made us dig deep for the win in a heart-stopping game that ended 30-25. I was being rested so André Pretorius wore the No 10 jersey but he had an off day, uncharacteristically missing a few kicks and not finding touch a few times. The Tongans were as fiery as the Samoans had been and the match turned into a wild roller coaster of brutal hits and thumping collisions. We were lucky to come away with a win and took this as a wake-up call that things can go horribly wrong very quickly at a World Cup.

Next we relocated to Montpellier in the south of the country to take on the United States at the Stade de la Mosson. This game was a special outing for me because I came up against one of my schoolmates from Maritzburg College, Chad Erskine, who was playing at scrumhalf. By way of a greeting I hit him with a hard tackle, perhaps slightly late, just to say howzit.

We scored nine tries to two and won the game 64-15. We didn't play with the precision we were hoping for but took the win. I also slotted two conversions, but the game will probably best be remembered for a try that was scored by the United States' Harare-born wing, Takudzwa Ngwenya, who hailed Bryan Habana as his rugby hero and then outdid him for pace on the outside to score a cracker.

The win over the Americans, our fourth straight victory, meant we had topped the log in our pool and lined us up for a quarter-final against Fiji, who were shock victors over Wales. The craziest results unfolded while we were in Marseille, as the two other favourites, New Zealand and Australia, were knocked out of the tournament by France and England respectively. It went completely against the run of play. No one saw it coming. We were bracing ourselves to play either of our Tri-Nations rivals in the final and with one fell swoop they were both gone!

We were watching the games on TV in our hotel rooms and there was quite a bit of noise with the guys excitedly shouting to each other out of the windows or down the passages as we watched both our main rivals tumble out of the tournament. This blew the competition wide open and from that moment on I knew we were in serious contention to win the World Cup – but not before we encountered an extremely close shave of our own.

My folks and brother had come over during the week to support us through the play-off stages, as did most of the other guys' families. We took on Fiji at the Stade Vélodrome in Marseille and were made to fight like world champions. The game could have ended in disaster, but Smitty held a tight rein and we showed composure when it was most needed to secure our passage to the semi-finals. Fiji had some big runners and the 55 600-strong crowd were supporting the underdogs big time! When Fiji sensed they could maybe steal a win they got their tails up and became hard to stop. We found ourselves level-pegging 20-20 deep into the game. While waiting behind our poles for a conversion attempt, Smitty started reading us the riot act, saying we hadn't come all this way and worked so hard over the past four years to go out like this. His words hit home and got me thinking of how bad it would be for my family, who had spent so much money and come all this way only to see us lose.

The other guys were of like mind and we slowly clawed our way out of the hole that we had dug. Monty put us back in front with a penalty and our forwards took the initiative to create the platforms for tries by Juan and myself. We eventually won 37-20 but don't let the score fool you – we were in trouble in that game. Luckily our experience and fighting spirit pulled us through.

Our semi-final opponents were Argentina, back in Paris at the Stade de France. The Pumas had an excellent flyhalf in Juan Martín Hernández, who I rated as one of the best I had come up against – he was well rounded and tough.

The game proved to be a bit of an arm wrestle, scrappy and niggly – just the way the Argentineans like it. At one point in the game I came up quickly and hit Hernández with a hard tackle, he rushed his pass and Bryan intercepted it to go and score under the poles. When I looked back from the tryline I could still see Hernández on the floor. It was a turning point for us in the game. We ended up winning 37-13 and were through to the final!

After the final whistle blew, Hernández came to our change room and asked if we could swap jerseys and when he took his jersey off, I could see a big red mark on his ribcage from where he'd been icing it due to the tackle.

So that was that. That was our journey to the 2007 Rugby World Cup final. It was a dream come true for us and the culmination of quite a journey.

Irish referee Alain Rolland got the final underway and just as in 1995, no tries were scored. All the points came from kicks and our victory was built on unrelenting tackling.

The forwards laid a solid foundation with great lineout work from Victor, Bakkies and Juan, while CJ, Smitty and Os applied themselves in the scrums, were very accurate and did not concede an inch. This was Os' swansong, his last game in the green and gold, and he stayed on the field for the full 80 minutes, becoming only the sixth player in World Cup history to earn two winner's medals. What a legend!

The loosies applied relentless pressure and as always, Schalk had a massive game, helped along by Danie and Juan. Fourie, Monty and I focused hard on being as accurate as possible with our kicking out of hand.

The only real close encounter we had was a touch-and-go decision by television match official Stuart Dickinson, which went our way. A piece of sloppy defence had allowed Mathew Tait to break through the midfield and when Monty missed him too, we were scrambling. The ball was moved to Mark Cueto on the left wing, and as he hurled himself at the line Danie put in a lifesaver – he didn't actually get to him properly, but his lunge caught Cueto's foot, causing him to brush the touchline near the corner.

The English bitched about it for a while afterwards, but I've looked at the tape numerous times and there is no doubt he was out. And even if he did score we all felt we had plenty in reserve to bounce back and play a more attacking game. We had kept it safe to secure a win; we had pumped this England side 36-0 a few weeks before and if we needed to play a more expansive game we could have. As it turned out, it wasn't necessary. Needless to say the match was what all World Cup finals should be – extremely tense.

I felt pure relief when the final whistle went. It was like years of pressure had just been lifted off our shoulders. It was awesome to know that we had actually done it and I'll never forget that moment when Smitty stepped up to receive the golden Webb Ellis Cup from the French president, Nicolas Sarkozy. Our president, Thabo Mbeki, was called into the team circle to share in the triumph. Fireworks went off and we were showered in little gold discs of confetti; everyone went bloody crazy.

We returned to the change room and soaked up the victory with cold beers and champagne. There was a jacuzzi in the room and we sat around having a few drinks, savouring this special moment. Jake was right, the golden cup was in our dressing room. Cameras were flashing and the corridor outside the room was packed with press guys clamouring for interviews.

I was told a guy from SuperSport called Tex (Teixeira) was in the passageway and wanted to interview me. When he asked me how we were going to celebrate I replied, 'We are going to be like Stevie Wonder and go all night long!' When I returned to the team and told Bob Skinstad what I'd said during the interview, Bob shook his head and replied: 'Lionel Richie sang that song you idiot!' I don't think I'll ever live it down, the guys still tease me about that.

Then it was out into the night with our special prize. Our fans were cheering, wanting to have pictures taken. The coach ride back to our hotel was over in a flash and a celebration of note broke out in our team room. All the guys' wives, girlfriends, close mates and family who had come over to support us joined in and we let rip. I might have got the singer's name wrong – but we did go all night long. I got to bed at about 6am the next morning.

It was awesome coming back to South Africa to a hero's welcome. It was completely crazy; there were thousands of people waiting for us at Johannesburg International. We went on a nationwide road show with the trophy a week or two later and it was madness. It felt like I'd gone from being an athlete to an alcoholic in the space of a week! It was function after function. People were so amazing in their support. We got to meet Madiba again – but this time with the trophy. I don't know if we heard him wrong, because he does talk in that unique way of his, but I'm sure he asked, 'Where's Hansie Pienaar?' Bless him, he might have said 'Francois Pienaar', I'm not too sure, but it was still awesome to meet him again.

At Newlands some nutter tried to snatch the trophy out of Bryan's hands while we were walking around the field. Imagine that, trying to nick the World Cup and thinking you can get away with it. He tried to make a run for it but didn't get very far before the security men were on to him; never forgetting that he was also being tailed by one of the fastest wings in world rugby!

The Springboks were nominated for the Team of the Year award at the prestigious Laureus World Sports Awards in the months following our successful World Cup campaign. The ceremony was held in St Petersburg in Russia, so Schalk, Monty, Bakkies, Bryan, Jake and I went over with our wives and girlfriends. It was an amazing ceremony, especially for someone like me who really loves his sport. It was awesome to meet some of the superstars of sport, like Roger Federer and Lewis Hamilton. 'The Fed', whose mother is South African, was very friendly towards us; we hung out and had a few photographs taken with him. And to top a wonderful experience we won the award, which was pretty cool.

This was my first experience of the Laureus World Sports Awards and since then I've become involved with them and their inspiring upliftment programmes. I've been to more ceremonies since and they're mind-blowing. The last one I went to was in Abu Dhabi in 2010 where the Boks were again nominated for the Team of the Year award, but lost out to the Brawn GP Formula One team.

That year, 2007, will always be etched in my memory as one of the greatest of my life. Jake, Smitty and the team delivered on our promise to the country and I will always be grateful for having experienced something as special as being part of a Springbok side that won a World Cup.

11

IT'S BATH TIME

ll good things must come to an end and 2008 provided me with a new set of challenges. The 2007 World Cup had come and gone and it was time for me to take stock of my career as a professional rugby player. My contract with the Sharks was due to come to an end just before the World Cup and there were no proactive moves on their part to renew. I was represented by the sports management company Prosport International and seeing as I had no desire to leave Kings Park my agent had approached the Sharks with the number for which I would be willing to put pen to paper. However, they came back with an offer that was quite a bit less than what I wanted so I was forced to look elsewhere.

Initially I considered Clermont Auvergne in Clermont-Ferrand, France, because John Smit was going there and told me the club was looking for a 10. As I didn't have a Springbok contract either, my agent and I had talks with Clermont during England's tour to South Africa. I was warming to the idea of going overseas so we also explored other avenues, commencing discussions with the English Premiership club

Bath RFC. Clermont came back to us before the Rugby World Cup and notified us that they were no longer in the market for a flyhalf so the decision, in effect, was made for me. I signed with Bath just before the World Cup started.

Not long after this the Sharks reverted to my agent with an offer that was higher than what we had originally requested but I had already signed on with Bath so it was too late. I was committed to Bath and therefore couldn't accept the Sharks' offer. Nevertheless, I was disappointed because first prize would have been to stay on and play for the Sharks.

Sometimes it's hard to come to terms with things while they're happening and I was quite upset with the guys at the Sharks but looking back now, I don't have any regrets that I went to Bath. Julia and I spent some very happy years in England. We were made to feel very welcome by the guys at the club as well as the locals. It was also an opportunity for Julia and me to experience a new environment and see a different part of the world. Bath is an extremely beautiful town. It's old and historic and being based there meant we were able to see wonderful parts of Europe we might not otherwise have visited.

I had heard a lot of positive things about Bath. The South African guys who had played there all had good things to say and the fact that an old mate from school, Pieter 'Dickie' Dixon, was there made the decision to sign for Bath a lot easier. My scrumhalf partner would be another South African, Michael Claassens. Michael and his wife Helen became special friends to Julia and me.

There's a club legend about another South African rugby player who had joined Bath a few years previously – a bloke by the name of Robbie Fleck. The story goes that after Fleckie decided to move from Western Province and the Stormers to further his career at Bath they put him up in the Holiday Inn for his first few nights. With no game to play for a few days Fleckie decided to take in the night spots of Bath and, as we say in KZN, things got a bit loose, so loose that he ended up stripping down naked and running around the Holiday Inn in all his glory. The staff were trying to contain this naked madman while wondering where this crazy South African had come from – only to see Fleckie don the Bath jersey the next weekend at centre! The story has probably been spiced up over the years and I might get a call from Fleckie to tell me off but it has become part of Bath's folklore.

The Recreation Ground at Bath enjoys one of the most picturesque settings in the rugby world. It nestles next to the River Avon, right in the heart of the city in the shadow of the Bath Abbey and Great Pulteney Street, with its attractive and historic old stone buildings. The Rec, as it is called by locals, is within walking distance of pubs and restaurants, ensuring a unique atmosphere on match days.

International stars such as Stuart Barnes, Jeremy Guscott, Jason Robinson, Phil de Glanville, Mike Catt and Mike Tindall had all donned the legendary blue, black and white of Bath rugby but the club had not had any silverware in its clubhouse for 10 years and were desperately trying to turn things around when I arrived. It was the kind of challenge I wanted to take on and I always played my heart out for Bath. In the few seasons I was there we reached the semi-finals of the English Premiership in May 2008, we won the European Challenge Cup in late May 2008, we reached the European Cup quarter-finals in April 2009, played the St George's Day game at Twickenham on 24 April 2010 in front of 60 208 people, and reached the Premiership semi-finals in May 2010.

I arrived in Bath a month before Julia did as I had to get there for rugby commitments. I got there on a Tuesday and played that Saturday, 10 November 2007, in my first fixture in my new strip. We were playing away so the road trip was a perfect opportunity to slot in and get to know the guys a bit better. I was fortunate to stay with Dickie at the home of another KZN boy, Matt Stevens, when I first arrived in Bath. The house was very spacious – something of a rarity in the UK – and we had some really good times there. I'll always be grateful to Matt for putting us up until Julia and I found our own place and settled in.

My first game for Bath was a memorable one against the French side Auch. It was played on a bitterly cold night, so cold you could see the steam every time you breathed out and you could hardly feel your toes. The conditions over there are really tough, but you have no choice but to get used to it. The game against Auch was our first match in the European Challenge Cup. I had a solid outing and scored a try in the 17th minute to contribute to our 28-6 victory and was happy to have got on the scoresheet in my first outing for the club.

My first season in the UK made me realise that we complain about the length and intensity of the South African season but the English boys play more often than we do.

Playing my rugby in England was very enjoyable but we were quite inconsistent. One day we'd be really strong and threatening and then a week later we'd fade, but I was enjoying my rugby big time and playing in a new set-up was fun, even though the rugby was non-stop. Clubs are involved in three competitions at once. It's hard on the body and it can become a bit of a blur. It takes a lot for the Poms to call off a fixture – they play in a foot of snow if necessary – and the groundsmen go to work with mops and rollers to ensure that games go on.

The arrival of some late April sunshine that year was most welcome and we beat the Sale Sharks 36-14 at The Rec to secure our place in the European Challenge Cup final, against Worcester at Kingsholm. But before we could focus on that match we had to concentrate on our progress in the Premiership. We met Gloucester in an afternoon of high drama. A win would have secured us a home semi-final, but we lost the game 6-8, meaning it was do or die against London Wasps at Adams Park the following week. However, our hopes of a place in the Premiership final were dashed as we went down 10-21.

The boys were gutted but we had to keep our heads up because we still had the European Challenge Cup final to play and couldn't allow this defeat to bring us down. We came up against a fired up Worcester side and for once the weather gave us a break. We ended the 10-year silverware drought for Bath rugby by winning 24-6. We were on top of the world and I was chuffed that my first season with Bath had ended so positively.

On the Springbok front, Jake White had been replaced as national coach by Peter de Villiers in a move containing heavy political overtones. It was surprising that Jake had not been asked to stay on; he had just won the World Cup and his results spoke volumes for his ability, but I'll address that later. The fact of the matter is that we had a new coach and were due to take on Six Nations champions Wales in a two-Test series in South Africa for the Prince William Cup.

I was very pleased to still be in the Springbok mix and we all met at a training camp in Cape Town before taking on the Welsh in the first Test in Bloemfontein. We provided the new coach with a perfect start by hammering the tourists 43-17. It was the first defeat Wales had been dealt since Warren Gatland took over as coach and I was pleased with my contribution – 23 points for landing five penalties and four conversions.

In the second Test at Loftus Wales were determined to demonstrate their status as the champions of Europe and put up a much better showing. We were trailing 20-21 going into the last quarter but managed to stage a late surge that carried us to a 37-21 victory. My kicking was still in the groove and I put 17 points on the board from four conversions and three penalties and it meant the Prince William Cup would keep the Webb Ellis Cup company in Saru's trophy cabinet at least until the year-end tour, when the Boks were scheduled to take on the Welsh at the Millennium Stadium in Cardiff.

The Springboks' next game was against Italy at Newlands the following Saturday. I had been given a rest and it was decided to give Frans Steyn a run at flyhalf. At the time there was a lot of talk of him being the next Bok No 10 but as it turned out, he struggled to come to terms with the demands of the position. To be fair, though, he was young and had already been shunted from position to position so making the transition to 10 in a Test match, even against Italy, was a big ask.

I hadn't really expected to be involved under Peter de Villiers, which was the case for a few of us, but I felt my all-round game had been good, while the old kicking foot had been right in the groove. However, being involved in the incoming Tests brought its challenges as I had my responsibilities to Bath to fulfil while also switching back into international mode for a one-off Test against Argentina and the 2008 Tri-Nations. Those were interesting times.

My second spell at Bath was as hectic as the first. It started off a little shaky but got better as the season progressed and I was grateful to our coach Steve Meehan when he gave me a two-week break after three months of what felt like 24-7 rugby. One of my most memorable games in a Bath jersey was around this time against the formidable Leicester Tigers. Former Blue Bulls mentor Heyneke Meyer was their coach and Derick Hougaard their No 10. This game was at home and went down to the wire. We stormed to a 20-3 lead in the first half but I don't know what Heyneke said to them at half-time because they came out like men possessed to wrest a 20-21 lead with just three minutes to go – precious seconds that stand out as one of my best memories of my time at Bath. I put a perfectly weighted kick across to our centre, Alex Crockett, and followed up. He made the catch and fed me an inside ball that put me in the clear for a memorable try. I missed the conversion but the delirium around The Rec was such that it barely mattered. We had won 25-21 and what made it even better is that some of my South African mates who were based in London were at the game and could join in the celebrations.

The season went along OK, we played some excellent rugby but as with the previous season, we also lost some games we should have won. I played virtually every game from November through to April 2009, until we got knocked out of the European Cup at Walkers Stadium on 11 April by an outstanding Leicester side. The British & Irish Lions were due to tour South Africa and I was hoping to be in the Bok mix when, you guessed it, my knee went! We were playing our last pool game of the Premiership against Newcastle when my rugby came to a shuddering halt. Yip … another flippin' knee injury to be followed by more surgery.

As I said, this was our last pool game and I was looking forward to a long break. However, fate dealt me a bad hand. Newcastle got a penalty and their scrummie took a quick tap. I was scuttling to get 10 metres back but he came straight at me; he stepped and I followed him. He changed direction and in trying to cut him down the angle was wrong and I heard that awful sound I had become all too familiar with.

The staff at Bath were amazing and got me set up with knee specialist Andy Williams, who works on a lot of the footballers' knees. I went to London for the surgery and then it was into the long recovery haul. This time it took nine months and believe me, it doesn't get any easier. Andy did an incredible job on the knee; I wish I'd met him earlier in my career as he was probably the best I'd experienced. The hospital was amazing but that may be because they had given me one of those contraptions that allow you to dose yourself with morphine to kill the pain. I was probably a little high half the time!

I stayed in England for the initial rehab and then returned to South Africa for some rest and time with the family; which is always good for recovery. I spent about a month or so at home before returning to Bath – where I started my long journey back to good health. The injury had happened in April 2009 and I was only going to be playing rugby again in January-February 2010.

The highs and lows; tell me about it. Talking of highs, the idyllic atmosphere at Bath was smashed by a drugs-related scandal that broke around the heads of the core of our top players. Word got out that some players were doing cocaine. Matt Stevens was the first to go; he was randomly tested during the season after a game, and after a positive test was banned from all rugby for two years. Matt was playing for England at the time and was a well-known personality in the UK – so to say the story was splashed all over the papers would be an understatement.

You would have thought the guys had learned their lesson from Matt's ordeal, but there was a furore that broke out at the end of the season because some of the guys took cocaine on our bus trip to London which marked the end-of-season celebrations. This caused a huge rift at Bath because one of the senior players went to the coaching staff and spilt the beans about the others. I was at home with my knee up at the time, so I wasn't even on the trip when the guys allegedly took the coke.

It caused a big division in the club because many felt the team spirit had been betrayed. I'm not saying that what they were doing was right, and I'm not advocating it in any way, but the guys who were involved and got into trouble always played hard and also knew how to have a good time … perhaps too much of a good time, but it could have been dealt with differently. The boys faced being hit with a massive fine, not to mention being banned from rugby for a very long time – career-threatening stuff – but in the end it panned out OK. It really was a disruption to the squad; we lost some quality players and it took a while for those of us left at Bath to gel and play as a tightly knit unit again.

Being injured again sucked but I did manage to keep myself busy. My agent, Christian Abt, had organised for me to go in to London to be part of a live panel during rugby games on Sky Sports and I enjoyed it because it gave me an opportunity to see some of my South African mates who were based in London. On one occasion we met for a quiet drink in Richmond. One drink turned into three or 30 and I eventually got to bed at about 3am. The only problem was that I was supposed to be on Sky Sports at about 6am for an international fixture so I only got about an hour and a half's sleep before appearing on national television. The mates I had spent the night with woke up too, just so that they could see what state I was in. They called me straight afterwards to give me gears and mock me about it, but I handled the show OK. Needless to say I couldn't wait for it to be over so I could get home and have a good kip!

Spending time in London was *lekker*. On one occasion Gregg Fry (Piggy), who became my mate when I tackled him in that game of domp at Maritzburg College, and Kevin Deana (Bones), had flown in from South Africa to listen to some mates of ours; who were in a band called The Shotguns and were playing a gig in South West London. It was a fantastic evening with loads of good friends; Rich Christer, Tom Attwood-Smith, Brad Barritt, Murray Marnoch and many others we hadn't seen for a while were there. We ended up getting very loose, as you do at a rock show. We *jolled* till the early hours and then met up again the next day for brunch in Putney at a quaint little place up on the hill called The Telegraph.

We partied into the night and then decided it was time to head into central London. On the way we called KP (Kevin Pietersen) and he suggested we join him at a club he was going to, but when we arrived the place was heaving and the queue was ridiculous, so I called him and said I didn't think we were going to get in. But he just said, 'No man, don't be stupid. I'll get Frankie to come and sort you okes out!' So we waited for this Frankie character to arrive and you can imagine our complete surprise when 'Frankie' turned out to be none other than Chelsea and England footballer Frank Lampard. He said 'hi' and escorted us into the club. It was quite funny because Lampard is Bones' hero and he spent the rest of the night saying 'Jiss, Frank is such a good oke, hey!' and we're like 'Take it easy Bones – the only thing he said was howzit!'

I made it back to playing rugby on 6 February 2010. I was chomping at the bit – half a chance to get back and play and I would be lacing on the boots. My first appearance came against the Sale Sharks at The Rec, a 40-minute spell that went well given how long I had been out of the game. One match report read: 'Well, he more than lived up to the billing, didn't he! Butch James' 40-minute cameo was remarkable not just for the variety and effectiveness of his distribution but also for the effect on the players around him.' It's always easier, though, when the team is playing well as a unit and we went on to win 40-7.

Bath had started the season badly but we managed to turn it around in the second half. Our third to last game against London Wasps at Twickenham was a real highlight. The match was watched by 60 208 spectators, who turned out for what was the St George's Day match in support of Help For Heroes. We won the game 35-19, earned a bonus point, and in the process gave Danny Grewcock something special to remember in his 200th appearance for the club.

The way we turned around our season was amazing. Even though we had lost six games in a row we still reached the semi-finals of the Premiership. It was a great adventure, but dreams of another grand day out at Twickenham were quickly put to rest as we got a rude awakening by slumping to a 6-15 defeat to the Leicester Tigers at Welford Road.

I was recalled to the Springbok squad in mid-2010 for home games against Italy and the Tri-Nations. I started at inside centre against Italy at the unusual venue of Witbank (the first Test ever played there) and came off the bench in four of the Tests against New Zealand and Australia. But bad luck continued to dog me and I ended up doing my shoulder against Australia at Loftus, which put me out of action for a few weeks before returning to England for my final season with Bath.

Joining Bath is one of the best decisions I ever made. The Bathonians were always supportive and hospitable. They are passionate about their team and really get behind you as a player if they see you're giving it your all. The club and its staff, from the coaching personnel to the administrators, were always good to me and for that I'll always be extremely grateful. I made some lifelong friendships and Bath will always have a special place in my heart.

Clockwise from left: Scoring against the All Blacks in the 2007 Tri-Nations; this was one of my best performances in a Bok jersey, against England at Twickenham in 2006; the Super 14 final against the Bulls in 2007; getting to grips with Victor Matfield in the final

Opposite page (clockwise from top left): With the legend, Os du Randt, after the 2007 World Cup final; my old Maritzburg College mate Chad Erskine, who played for the USA in the 2007 World Cup; Smitty and me with the greatest prize in rugby
This page: In action for the Boks during the 2007 World Cup, definitely the greatest highlight of my career

Opposite page (from top): The squad celebrating our World Cup victory with a few cold ones; my family joined in the celebrations after the final *This page (clockwise from left):* With Roger Federer at the 2008 Laureus World Sports Awards; the Stade de France, minutes after we had won the World Cup final; Percy Montgomery, Schalk Burger, Jake White, Bakkies Botha, Bryan Habana and me after we won the trophy for the World Team of the Year at the Laureus World Sports Awards. The ceremony took place in St Petersburg, Russia

Opposite page (clockwise from top left): On holiday in the Transkei, taking a 'fine'!; New Year's at the end of 2006 with 'Tucky', 'Razor', 'Piggy' and me; Julia and me at the wedding of Deon Carstens and his wife Hildegard; Monty, Smitty, Bob Skinstad and me outside our hotel in Paris in 2007; we managed to take a trip to Disneyland in Paris during the 2007 World Cup

This page (clockwise from right): Recovering in hospital the day after my last knee op; Craig Davidson and me at Joe Cools in Durban. The toothpicks always come out after a few drinks!; the naughty team that was put together for New Year's at the end of 2006; the scars from my fifth ACL reconstruction

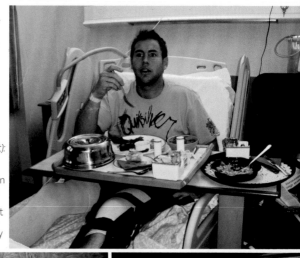

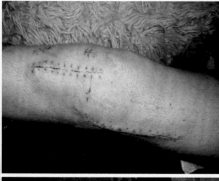

Julia and me on our special day

12

BOARDROOM BATTLES

Although Jake White guided us to victory in the 2007 Rugby World Cup in France there was quite a bit of tension behind the scenes. Jake was good at insulating us from the rugby politics but we were aware that there was strife between him and the South African Rugby Union (Saru) and on occasion he mentioned that he was not keen to stay on as coach. In the flush of victory he started to reconsider but relations between him and Saru had broken down to such an extent that the partnership couldn't continue.

During my first spell with Bath I received word that Saru had decided it would not renew Jake White's contract as national coach because he had not reapplied for the post. I think this really annoyed Jake as he was probably expecting to at least be asked whether he wanted the job or not, even though he might have declined the offer. By then Jake was so sick of the meddling administrators and the politics involved that he was happy to leave while he was on top, which is usually the best time to go.

There had been a lot of pressure on Jake; he had a lot to deal with off the field and there was so much intrigue behind the scenes that I made the conscious decision not to get involved and to keep my head down and play rugby. As a Bok No 10 you have enough to worry about without getting involved in stuff you have no control over and which has nothing to do with what happens on the field of play.

One of the biggest issues during Jake's tenure came from the controversy around then Stormers loose forward Luke Watson, and I found myself feeling sorry for Luke. He never held a gun to anyone's head to make them select him and in a way was also a victim of processes he had no control over. In my opinion, he was as angry as everyone else about the way his selection to the Springbok side came about, because it tarnished what was meant to be something special. Luke is serious about his rugby and I'm sure he would have loved to play for the Boks on his merits, rather than with Jake being instructed to include him. OK, he was caught out saying he felt like puking on the Springbok jersey, which was wrong, but it probably came from him being frustrated and sick of dealing with so many off-field issues.

We were at a Bok camp in Bloemfontein and some of the senior guys were unhappy at the way Luke had been drafted in (by decree of Saru president Oregan Hoskins) for the match against Samoa, and were hostile towards him. It was a pity because Luke has a good rugby brain on his shoulders, and plays the game hard. In the end he got so sick of the in-fighting and hidden agendas in SA rugby that he moved to Bath, where we became team-mates again – we were team-mates and housemates in our very early days at the Sharks.

It was a good move for him to get away from the politics and be in an environment where he could enjoy his rugby. Luke is a great leader and is passionate about this game. Julia and I became good friends with Luke and his wife Elaine, and spent some good times with them in Bath.

In the meantime, Jake was gone and Saru then made the historic decision to appoint South Africa's first black coach in Peter de Villiers. It feels wrong to even talk in this vein because the colour of a person's skin makes no difference to me but unfortunately it is a South African reality and as I lived through a time of change in Springbok rugby I should document it.

I first came into contact with Peter at the Springbok training camp ahead of our Test series against Wales in South Africa in 2008. At the time, with Jake having moved on, I thought my days as the Springboks' first-choice flyhalf were numbered; more so because the new coach had made it clear he would not be picking anyone based overseas. However, my form at Bath had been good and I got a call from Peter saying he wanted me to attend the training camp in Cape Town. I was surprised but very happy to be back in the mix with the Boks.

Peter had also appointed new assistant coaches in Dick Muir (backline) and Gary Gold (forwards) and it did take a little getting used to, but the presence of a lot of senior players from Jake's era made the transition a little easier. Peter definitely leaned on the senior players and took their input and suggestions on board to get the ship sailing.

In Cape Town I had my first experience of Peter and his somewhat unpredictable ways. He'd made no secret about the fact that Stormers pivot Peter Grant (Bash) was going to be his first-choice flyhalf. He ran Bash in the starting line-up when I arrived and continued to do so for the first few practices, before suddenly making a U-turn and telling me I was going to be the No 10 in the run-on team.

It came as a shock as I'd accepted that I would play a supportive role and that Bash would wear the No 10 jersey. It was awkward at practice when Peter called him over and had a chat to him, obviously telling him that he wasn't going to start anymore. I felt really bad for Bash because I could see how disappointed he was. It was his chance to get his foot in the door. He was playing really good rugby at the time and given the chance he may very well have ensconced himself in the side.

That's what happens at this level. There are some 50 million people in South Africa but only 15 guys can run on to represent the country so when you get that one chance you have to take it with both hands. Sadly Bash never really got that chance. He's such a good guy; and was a few years below me at Maritzburg College. It was tough but I had to grab the opportunity Peter had passed my way (I wouldn't turn down a chance to play for the Boks even if it was at tighthead prop) but I did feel bad for Bash that day.

Peter's first Test in charge was played in Bloemfontein, just as Jake's and Rudolf Straeuli's had been. As mentioned in the previous chapter, I managed to turn in two good performances against the Welsh, scoring 23 points in the first Test and 17 points in the second Test before being asked to stand down for the match against Italy. I was retained for the Tri-Nations.

We started our away leg of the competition against the All Blacks in Wellington. It turned out to be a tough old day at the office after a shocking incident involving John Smit and All Blacks lock Brad Thorn as early as the sixth minute. The whistle had already gone when Thorn lifted Smitty, tipped him, and forced him head first into the ground. Tackles like that have come to be known as 'spear' or 'tip' tackles and it was plain dirty. The incident happened right in front of referee Stuart Dickinson and we were incensed that he didn't reach for a card. Smitty tried to soldier on but eventually had to go off in the 37th minute because of the injury he had suffered in the tackle.

To make matters worse their No 10, Dan Carter, had a great game tactically, keeping us pinned in our own half, but we fought hard and scored a try just before the break.

It wasn't enough, though, and in the end we lost the game 8-19; we were lucky we didn't lose by more.

With the Tri-Nations having been extended to include an extra game against the Kiwis and the Aussies, we faced the daunting prospect of taking on the rampant All Blacks at Carisbrook in Dunedin – New Zealand's famous 'House of Pain'. We were not given much of a chance, but we had the belief that we could do it. We knew we hadn't played well in Wellington the week before and knew that if we played to our potential we could take the All Blacks. We ended up proving the old axiom that a wounded Springbok is a dangerous animal.

As always in a Springboks-All Blacks Test every metre of space was fiercely contested. Carter kicked four penalties to Percy Montgomery's three but then we struck an important blow by getting the first try – Joe van Niekerk peeling off the back of a scrum to put JP Pietersen in. That gave us a 14-12 lead and I got the chance to stretch it to 17-12 when the ball came back smoothly and I had the time to slot a drop. Carter cut our lead with another penalty just before the break (17-15) and that seemed to galvanise the All Blacks because they really came at us after the re-start. Our defence held until the 56th minute but Conrad Smith managed to eke out some space and put replacement flank Sione Lauaki in for a try that Carter converted to give the All Blacks the lead, 17-22. Next Leon MacDonald was penalised for a high tackle on Bryan Habana and I managed to steer over the kick to make the difference just two points.

We were going at it hammer and tongs when Carter, breaking his usual pattern, evaded a couple of tacklers and steadied himself to drop a goal, making the score 20-25, but another penalty allowed me to cut the difference back to two points shortly afterwards. We were starting to believe we might pull it off when we suffered a massive blow; Victor Matfield was yellow-carded by referee Matt Goddard for a high tackle on Lauaki just as we were going into the last 10 minutes. Carter kicked the ensuing penalty to make it 23-28 and with time running out the crowd were starting to celebrate another victory for the All Blacks in their South Island stronghold.

With just 14 men on the field it wasn't looking good when out of nowhere Ricky Januarie took the opportunity to write his name into the history books. We were in our own half when Ricky spotted a pair of front-row forwards blocking his way and conjured up a try out of nothing. He broke, chipped over the head of the advancing MacDonald, made no mistake when recollecting the ball and launched himself over the line for a glorious try. That tied the scores at 28-28 and, with both Monty and me having been subbed, Frans Steyn showed what he is made of by blocking out memories of the Super 14 final the year before and slotting the conversion to put us two points clear. The All Blacks threw the kitchen sink at us, Carter missed a drop goal attempt and Ma'a Nonu crashed forward dangerously but we held on for a famous victory.

Beating the All Blacks in New Zealand is massive. This was the Boks' first ever win in Dunedin, and the Boks' first tour there was in 1921. It was only the second time we had beaten the All Blacks in New Zealand since the 1998 Tri-Nations.

Unfortunately we couldn't maintain the momentum in our next game against the Wallabies at the Subiaco Oval in Perth. The final score was only 9-16 but we were outscored two tries to nil as Lote Tuqiri and Stirling Mortlock got over our line and Matt Giteau and Berrick Barnes (with a drop) trumped the three penalties Frans and I contributed.

Next up was a Nelson Mandela tribute match against Argentina at Ellis Park that had been slotted into the fixture list to celebrate Madiba's 90th birthday. It was our first meeting with the Pumas since the World Cup semi-final 10 months previously and there was additional attention on the Argentineans because it had recently been announced that Sanzar was looking at adding them to an expanded Tri-Nations. We started off a little slowly, but then turned it on for Madiba, to run up a new record score against Argentina – who were missing a lot of first-choice players. The 54-point margin surpassed the 31-point margin at the Estadio Ferrocarril Oeste in Buenos Aires set back in 1996. We scored nine tries to nil and I was chuffed to have landed all nine conversions.

Whipping the Pumas seemed like the perfect way to prepare for the home leg of the Tri-Nations – especially as the return Test against the All Blacks at Newlands was a significant occasion. Monty was set to become the first Springbok to reach 100 Test caps and Peter de Villiers had left him out of the Argentina game to ensure that he reached this remarkable milestone at his beloved home ground. Unfortunately, though, we were unable to present Monty with a victory to go with the golden cap he had received to mark the occasion. Nothing went right; we ended up being thumped 0-19 and I can tell you that few things hurt more than seeing that big fat zero on the scoreboard.

The Wallabies were waiting for us in Durban and the hangover of going down to the All Blacks continued as we slumped to a 15-27 defeat. It was a loss that ended our hopes in the tournament and it wasn't nice being reminded that this was the first time Australia had won on South African soil in eight years.

People were now talking about the demise of the world champions and that put a cracker up our backsides for the final game of the tournament at Ellis Park in Johannesburg. The Wallabies might have been a bit complacent but we dealt it to them that afternoon, running in eight tries in a record 53-8 victory. Jongi Nokwe became the first Springbok to score four tries in a Test against Australia and people started talking about a new expansive game being played by the

Boks. However, I didn't really go along with that because to me it was just Springbok rugby at its best – hard, physical, doing the basics right, impenetrable in defence and ruthless on attack. It was a great way to end off the tournament.

There's no rest for the wicked in pro rugby and soon I was on the plane back to Bath for the 2008-09 'Christmas season' and, as previously mentioned, that's when my knee went again. It was a helluva blow – not only because of the torturous road to recovery but because it knocked me out of contention to play against the British & Irish Lions, who were returning to South Africa in 2009. Lions tours only come by every 12 years so it hurt to know I would not be adding one of those bright red jerseys to the collection of teams I had won caps against.

Mulling over my notes while writing this book I found some of Dr Andrew Williams' comments with regards to the knee injury that kept me from playing against the Lions. They'll give you an idea of the extent of the injury and how close I came to having my career ended.

'Butch has had four previous ACL reconstructions (two in each knee). The left knee had a hamstring graft when it first had an ACL rupture but this failed. His last ACL reconstruction involved prosthetic ligaments, which did function well for a few years. Unfortunately, he then had a subluxation episode and the MRI has confirmed a re-rapture of the graft. Since the beginning of the year he has been struggling with swelling. I explained the nature of the problem to him, emphasising that he has established, known chondral (cartilage) damage. I explained that with his history and the fact that he does have serious chondral damage, that he should consider abandoning further ACL reconstructions and therefore also his rugby playing career. Butch has, however, made it clear that he is keen to get back to rugby, although he has accepted there is a real risk that despite further surgery, he might not return to the game.'

That was in early 2009. I had the op with Dr Williams at the Chelsea & Westminster Hospital, missed the Lions tour, went back to playing for Bath almost a year later and then clawed my way back into the Springbok mix again.

As if tearing the inside of my knee to pieces and missing out on the Lions tour wasn't enough, I ended up coming back into the fold during 2010, playing some good rugby for Bath, being recalled to the Springboks and then popping my shoulder out in my second game back for the Boks. And to top it all off I had another set of disappointing negotiations with Sharks commercial manager Rudolf Straeuli and CEO Brian van Zyl, which was a real pity because I was keen to pull a Sharks jersey over my head again.

I joined up with the Boks on 19 June 2010 to play Italy in Witbank. We won ugly, 29-13, against former Bok coach Nick Mallett's Italians, with Peter giving me a run at No 12. The coaches were taking a long-term view towards the 2011 World Cup and checking how I would cope in case problems arose in that position – if Jean de Villiers got injured, for instance. The idea was to see if I could cover 10 and 12.

There were a couple of unfamiliar faces in the squad but my joy at being back was tempered when I got yellow-carded for a high tackle on Italy fullback Luke McLean. And boy did this give the critics something to shout about. I had hardly been in trouble in this area of my game for ages, but one loose tackle and all hell breaks loose. There were some write-ups that said my reputation would come back to haunt the Boks and that I would cost them the World Cup in 2011. One or two called for my head and said I should be replaced in the Bok set-up. I knew the tackle wasn't that bad and I wasn't suspended, which meant I could come on as a sub in the following week's game in East London when the team kicked up a gear and beat Italy 55-11.

The Boks then went on their away leg of the Tri-Nations. With Bulls No 10 Morné Steyn having become the preferred choice at flyhalf, I didn't make the starting line-up in any of the fixtures but did add to my tally of caps by twice coming off the bench. We were pumped 12-32 by the All Blacks in Auckland, 17-31 in Wellington a week later and then 13-30 by the Wallabies at the Suncorp Stadium in Brisbane.

The resumption of the Tri-Nations against the All Blacks was a big occasion in the annals of Springbok rugby. It was scheduled to be played in Soweto at the massive Soccer City just a month after the Fifa World Cup final had been staged there and to top it all off, it was to be Smitty's 100th Test. The Boks gave it their all to do it for him (I was on the bench but didn't get into the action) and it seemed the occasion would be marked by a famous victory with us leading 22-17 with about 10 minutes left to play.

The clock ticked down agonisingly slowly with the record 94 700 crowd on the edge of their seats but we were denied in the cruellest fashion. Richie McCaw got over for a try in the right corner in the 78th minute to level the scores, and then on the stroke of full-time the All Blacks won a turnover, surged up the middle, and worked Israel Dagg over for a try in the opposite corner. Carter converted to make it 22-29 and my heart just bled for Smitty. Typically, he blamed himself: 'At 22-22 the plan was to have a crack with the ball in hand and get Morné into the pocket. But we suffered a turnover and then I missed a tackle and that was the game over. I can't physically describe how it feels to lose your 100th game because of your own missed tackle.'

The next game was against the Wallabies at Loftus and we broke a string of losses by winning 44-31. This was a special occasion for Victor Matfield – his 100th Test at his beloved Loftus Versfeld. I came on in the second half and put in a tackle late in the game that left me with a subluxation of my shoulder (a partial dislocation). It couldn't have come at a worse time because we were hard on attack trying to close out a see-saw game that had seen us concede a pair of tries, to Will Genia and Matt Giteau, in the first five minutes to trail 0-14. I kept swinging my arm in the hope that the shoulder would pop back in and tried to keep up with play. A strong run by Pierre Spies put us hard on attack and good work by Victor and Jean provided the handling touches that got JP in for the game-clinching try. With Morné off the field the conversion was mine to take and while waiting to place the ball I told the doctor I would not be able to continue if play went on after the kick. I took my time, guided the ball between the uprights to seal our 44-31 win, and was happy to hear the final whistle go as the flags went up.

It was a nice way to end the game but I couldn't believe my bad luck at having popped the shoulder, because I had been told there was a good chance I would start the following week against the Wallabies in Bloemfontein. As it turned out, that would be my last involvement with the Boks for the year.

The time had come to be patched up before I could get back in the saddle. I saw a consultant orthopaedic surgeon, Dr Jennings, and his diagnosis didn't make for good reading. I had an MRI scan done after the injury which, according to Dr Jennings, revealed an 'anterior labral detachment and also marked thinning of the supraspinatus testing with some delamination'.

I went ahead with a complex shoulder arthroscopy to repair the joint at the Hospital of St John and St Elizabeth in St John's Wood in London during September 2010, with Dr Wallace as the lead surgeon. The restriction to the range of movement was cleared by mid-October at which point I could start using an exercise bike, do some theraband strengthening and start running again. I started playing again at the turn of the year for what was to be my farewell spell with Bath.

My mindset had changed, though, and I found myself longing to get back to South Africa again. The year 2011 was obviously a Rugby World Cup year and I knew that if I wanted to maximise my chances of making the squad, I'd have to be playing in South Africa. Julia and I had started to miss our friends and family, but most of all I wanted to end my career back at home. Being hurt again, I had come to the conclusion that if I picked up one more injury I'd stop playing. I know I'd thought that before but this time I really did mean it and that intensified my desire to get back to South Africa. I mentioned this to my agent and we started putting out feelers to a few SA unions.

Contractual issues can be quite complicated so allow me to sketch some of the background for you. I had signed a two-year contract with Bath in 2007, which would expire in 2009. However, after the 2008 season Bath wanted to extend my contract for another three years, up to 2011. I felt that might be a bit long so I agreed to sign for another two years, with the option to take on a third year if I felt I was up to it. Bath were agreeable but added that they wanted the option after the two years was up to be able to release me should I be playing poorly. I was fine with that.

My agent and Bath then agreed that I would play another two seasons and if I wanted to go home and play after that it would be fine. Bath's only condition was that I couldn't play for anyone else in the Premiership – at least that's what I thought I had agreed to – and it was a huge mistake on my behalf to not see the contract in writing and signed.

My lure was in the water and one of the nibbles came from Rudolf Straeuli at the Sharks. My agent and I started chatting to him with an eye to my coming back to Durban and healing the rift that had developed between us from our previous negotiations when I still had two seasons left on my contract with Bath.

What had happened, in late 2009, was that the Sharks had no flyhalves for the beginning of their 2010 Super Rugby campaign. Their new signing – Juan Martín Hernández, had just injured his back and Pat Lambie had not yet come to the fore in the No 10 jersey. It was the end of 2009 and I had come out to South Africa for a short break. One afternoon I went to watch a Sharks practice and had a chat to the coach John Plumtree and assistant coach Grant Bashford about the possibility of having a run for the Sharks. They were desperate and I was willing to play. John and Grant form a great coaching team and I was up to the challenge and hungry to play some Super Rugby for the Sharks.

But I first had to square things with Bath. I had been injured for half of Bath's season but had made my way back nicely from the knee injury. Bath had lost a string of games and there seemed very little hope of making any play-offs, so when the Sharks started speaking to me, I spoke to Bath, telling Steve Meehan, the coach, that if Bath were to be knocked out of the Premiership, I'd like the opportunity to play for the Sharks on a loan basis. Bath, however, were not keen on the idea and said that we had to try and at least make the top six to qualify for the European Cup the following season. As I was still contracted to Bath my obligation lay with them, so I said it was fine and we left it at that. I was still very keen to play for Bath as well, so I gave up hope of having a few outings with the Sharks and let the coaching staff at Bath know it was all systems go.

I went back to Bath and we miraculously turned our season around, ending up in the semis. The Sharks, however, kept on talking to my agent and the exchanges continued to go to and fro throughout 2010. At the start of the 2011 season the Sharks again showed an interest in me. I was very keen to return to Durban and was excited at the prospect. Rudolf and I chatted a few times and he said that he would be talking to the board to see if we could come to some sort of agreement. He came back to me and said that the board had agreed to everything he and I had discussed. I was very excited because Rudolf said the deal was 90% in the bag.

Rudolf really got my hopes up but the call to confirm our arrangement never came. We tried to find out what was going on and that's when Brian van Zyl got involved, saying he wasn't happy with the transfer fee that I felt had been agreed upon and that he wasn't going to pay it. Brian declared that when I left the Sharks in 2007 to move to Bath the Sharks had not received a transfer fee. But why should they have? I didn't have any fixtures left for the Sharks, we had no games left on my contract, so to my mind I was a free agent. In fact, my contract with the Sharks actually ended in December, but they stopped paying me in October.

Brian and Rudolf then stated that I was asking too much, which I found astonishing as Rudolf and I had come to an agreement on the details. He had not questioned the price and had in fact assured me that everything was perfectly fine, so somewhere along the line there was a classic case of 'broken telephone' and maybe I should have spoken to Brian directly to avoid all of this in the first place. As a consequence Alistair McArthur of the Sharks' sponsor, Mr Price, organised a meeting between himself, Rudolf, Brian and me, in an attempt to rescue the situation and to see if there was any way we could work something out. I was quite upbeat and feeling positive that Alistair might be able to help us find some middle ground.

However, the meeting didn't go too well. Brian and Rudolf started raising a whole lot of issues about my 2007 season at the Sharks. They brought up how many times I had been injured and how much game time I'd had and how much money they'd spent on me. They hauled out a batch of documents and figures to make their point, when in actual fact I was simply there to try and see if there was any way in which we could come to an agreement on a deal moving forward. They were aggrieved that in spite of everything the Sharks had done for me I had left them in the lurch in 2007, which was crazy because I wanted to stay. The reason I had left then was because the Sharks made no effort to keep me. I would have been more than happy to put a clause in my contract that stated they wouldn't have to pay me if I got injured again, as I was so keen to return. I wanted to resolve whatever issues there were because anyone who knows me knows how passionate I am about the Sharks. It was a little bizarre, to say the least, and I'm sad that it became so unpleasant because playing for the Sharks is something I hold close to my heart.

Salvation eventually came from an unlikely quarter when the Lions made me an offer. Some good people, like Eric Ichikowitz, made sure that the deal went through and I became a Lion. Eric handles a lot of the recruiting and contracts at the Lions and also plays a significant role as one of the directors at Gilbert. He is also brother to Ivor Ichikowitz – who partnered with another local businessman, Robert Gumede, to obtain shares in the Lions' set-up – sadly an arrangement that subsequently went sour. Playing for the Lions was something I had never thought of throughout my career, but when the opportunity arose it made sense and I was motivated from day one to pull the Lions jersey over my head with pride and give something back to the Ichikowitz brothers, who had really come through for me.

13

PART OF
THE PRIDE

Signing up with the Lions was what you would call a rugby-changing experience but I had other life-changing events happen during this passage of my life. I married my long-time sweetheart, Julia Westbrook, daughter to Mike and Ingrid Westbrook and sister to Lucy Westbrook. Mike is a well respected doctor in Kloof and still runs his practice there. I really couldn't have asked for a better bride or better in-laws and am really blessed to have such great people in my life.

Julia and I were married at Lynton Hall in Pennington on the KwaZulu-Natal south coast on 5 February 2011 – just a few months before I put pen to paper with the Lions and shortly before we moved back from the UK for good. We had a fabulous wedding in the company of 230 friends and family. It was such a special day. Julia and I had been dating for almost eight years and she had been with me through all my ups and downs. I owe her a lot for being so patient throughout the years that rugby dominated my life. Julia's had to nurse me through my operations, which often left me incapable of doing even the simplest things. She's been a pillar of strength and the perfect companion. I couldn't have wished to have anyone better by my side, so marrying her was a special and proud moment in my life.

Elton was my best man and lived up to his title. My groomsmen were Gregg Fry and Peter Cameron and my MC was Kevin Deana, all guys who had walked the walk with me from the time we met at Maritzburg College. Julia and I went for our honeymoon – to the Maldives – a month after the wedding because of rugby commitments at Bath – and I can truly say that it's the most amazing place I have ever been to. We stayed in a small resort called Medhufushi for nine nights but would have stayed for nine months if we could have! We tanned, swam, snorkelled, ate great food and just chilled out. We stayed in a villa on the water and had romantic dinners on the beach prepared by our own private chef – the perfect way to start married life together.

Soon, though, it was back to business. I had to finish my last few games at Bath and then race to join the Lions, who were about to tour New Zealand and Australia in Super Rugby. The Lions came through for me just at the right time. Julia and I had really enjoyed our time at Bath. We met some amazing people, it was great to experience club rugby abroad and we made some fantastic friends.

However, I wanted to come home to South Africa and give it one last crack. The Lions gave me a good contract; I paid half my transfer fee but was happy to take the knock. Seeing that I was born in Johannesburg it meant I had come full circle. An added bonus was that Elton is based in Joburg too.

I immediately liked the mixed environment in the Lions set-up – a lot of young talent with a couple of guys who had been around the block. They had placed a lot of faith in me so I was determined to deliver on the field for them. We were able to sort the contractual stuff out pretty fast but nothing like as quick as slotting into the team. I left

England on the Tuesday, arrived in Joburg, went to pick up my Lions kit and then went straight back to OR Tambo International Airport to board a plane to Australia. I arrived on Thursday, had a captain's run on the Friday and sat on the bench for the game on the Saturday. Being on the road helped me to get to know the guys fast and we gelled quickly.

It's definitely the best thing to slot into a new team while you're on tour. You get an opportunity to build team spirit because you see the guys all the time, whereas at home the guys come to practice and then leave straight afterwards. There may be the odd dinner or braai, but on tour you get to hang out 24-7. Slotting in at the Lions was easy; there's a great bunch of guys there. I obviously knew Wikus van Heerden from our Baby Bok days, right up to the World Cup in France, while Pat Cilliers and Michael Rhodes were former team-mates from the Sharks. It was very easy to slot in. The guys in the team were most welcoming and I immediately felt at home.

That first time I pulled a Lions jersey over my head was in Canberra for our game against the Brumbies. The Lions staged a magnificent turnaround to score one of their best overseas victories, winning the game 29-20. The previous week the Lions had shipped 50 points against the Cheetahs but John Mitchell cracked the whip, made 10 changes, and got the kind of performance he was looking for. I got my first taste of action in the next game against the Waratahs in Sydney. We let in a soft try about 90 seconds into the game which allowed the Tahs to get their tails up and we slid to a 12-29 defeat. Our best moment was a counter-attack that started on our own 22m line and ended with a try by Jaco Taute at the other end – made possible by quick ball that came back to me with the Tahs' defence stretched. I was able to put through a grubber which the talented young fullback raced on to. Unfortunately, this was the last time we came close to taking the lead or upsetting the Waratahs' applecart.

Our next fixture was against the Highlanders in Dunedin and it was decided I would play at inside centre. It's not my preferred position if I have to be honest, but I'm happy to fill in anywhere if it's going to add value and on this occasion it was well worth it as I played a support role to young Elton Jantjies, who turned in a superb performance. We shocked the Highlanders, who were looking good to reach the play-offs, by winning 26-22. My old mate Wikus was the hero of the hour; with his head covered in bandages and blood seeping from a wound, he drove through the Highlanders' defence in the 79th minute to give us our third win of the season and our second on tour. The win meant a lot to us, as summed up by our captain Doppies la Grange when he said: 'I've played for the Lions for a very long time and I can't remember us winning in New Zealand, so it's a big occasion for us.'

We were looking for our third win on tour the following week, but had very few answers to the Hurricanes' attack. We dominated in the early parts of the game but we let ourselves down defensively. That being said, we showed that we had a lot of fight in us and it was certainly a good character builder for the side. Having guys like Ma'a Nonu running at you means you have to have your defensive wits about you. I played inside centre again and Elton played at 10. We threw the kitchen sink at it in the dying minutes but it wasn't enough and we went down 27-38.

The mood was happy on the long haul back to Joburg because even though there had been defeats, the Lions had never previously won two games on tour, so there were positive vibes that the hard work being done and a new attitude was starting to pay off.

Our next outing was strange for me as it came against the Sharks. I never thought I would one day turn out against my old home province, and as it turned out, fate left me with something to remember the occasion by. The Sharks were 30-9 down but clawed their way back to level the scores. It was an enthralling game and the Sharks had to be admired for their fighting spirit, but in the end they had me to thank for giving them a helping hand. It was one of those days where everything seemed to be going right; I felt I was controlling the game and was enjoying giving it one to my old team-mates, but during the second half Sharks flank Keegan Daniel tried to break past me and in a reflex action I stuck my arm out and hit him a bit high. There was no malicious intent; it was a split second instance, which can happen in rugby. I was shown a yellow card and in the 10 minutes I was off the field the momentum shifted to the Sharks. Needless to say I got a three-week suspension.

It was great being back on South African soil and settling into Joburg was not as difficult as I thought it might be. Richmark Holdings CEO Gavin Varejes was kind enough to let Julia and I stay in his apartment while we found a place of our own to settle into. We appreciated Gavin's generosity because it gave us a little bit of breathing space; Julia could feel safe and secure in a new city as I had to leave her on her own before flying out to Australia. The life of the wife of a professional sportsman can be quite daunting. Knowing someone was keeping an eye out for Julia certainly gave me peace of mind so a big thank you to Gav and his wife Jo-Ann for helping to make the move a smooth one.

I got a call from Peter de Villiers while I was on tour with the Lions. He had rung me up towards the latter part of 2010 when I was still in Bath and told me that he'd like me to come back to South Africa. With the World Cup in mind, Andy Marinos, Saru's manager of national teams, also came over to speak to a few overseas-based players such as Ruan Pienaar, Frans Steyn and me, as well as our respective clubs, to try and get us back to South Africa.

Getting a call from the Bok coach isn't something that happens every second day, so I was pleased to hear him on the phone and also to be told that he was planning to take me to the World Cup in New Zealand and that I was going to be his No 1 flyhalf. He added that I mustn't do anything silly or get injured. That's when I knew for the first time that I'd be going to the 2011 World Cup.

Peter's call really lifted my spirits, especially as it came during a break in which I had time to recharge, give the knees a bit of a rest and catch up with some business. I'd invested in an advertising agency based in Durban called Sugar at the beginning of 2010. I'm proud to say that I'm one of the founding members and a director. The idea of starting an ad agency came about in 2009 while I was still in Bath. Warren Haviside had previously been a senior creative at TBWA Hunt Lascaris before moving to London to take up a position as a senior copywriter at a London-based agency called Inferno. Warren had been a school mate of mine at Maritzburg College and he and my brother-in-law Gregg Fry, who at the time was an account executive at TBWA in Durban, paid me a visit in Bath. We started talking about my plans after rugby and I fell back on my usual joke about being a car guard. However, the conversation steered towards more serious matters when Gregg and Warren mentioned they wanted to break away from the big agencies they were working for and proposed that I should think about joining them. The idea was that I would carry on playing rugby while they started an agency, which would leave me with a possible career path and the option of joining them full time once my playing days came to an end.

Sugar made a solid start to life and won some notable accounts. The team has expanded and we've launched a production arm called Sugar Productions – which facilitates the shooting of stills and TV commercials in and around Durban and outlying areas like the Transkei, Lesotho, the Midlands, the north coast and Mozambique, which have amazing locations. The boys have done some great production jobs and facilitated and produced a couple TV commercials, numerous stills shoots as well as a Jockey International campaign. It's comforting to know the guys are keeping the ship afloat so I can concentrate on rugby while they carry on with the business.

I really enjoyed my little excursions into a life outside rugby but soon it was time to allow the Sugar crew to return to their Apple Macs while I returned to Joburg to pack my bags for two weeks of reconditioning and fitness with technical adviser Rassie Erasmus and Springbok team doctor Derik Coetzee, or 'Doc Derik' as we call him.

A lot of the senior players were rested for the away leg of the Tri-Nations. We were taken to Rustenburg to go through a conditioning programme and to work on structures and game plans under Rassie while Peter took charge of the touring team. The same kind of thing happened under Jake White in 2007 and the logic was still relevant – that the World Cup is more important than the Tri-Nations and that the away leg could be used to see which of the guys on the fringes of the squad could use the opportunity to play themselves into (or out of) the World Cup squad.

Rassie had also been part of the 2007 World Cup build-up and he's no slouch when it comes to putting the guys through their paces. He worked us hard at fitness sessions while a lot of attention was paid to rehabilitating whatever injuries we might have been struggling with. I'd battled with swelling on both my knees for a number of years after games or heavy sessions so the camp was important for a guy like me. It also gave the senior players a chance to bond again after playing for our respective clubs and unions.

The away leg of the Tri-Nations didn't go too well and the Boks drew plenty of flak from the media and fans, but in all honesty it went exactly the way it did in 2007. It was always going to be less than perfect with the core of the starting line-up staying home and the coaching staff trying out new combinations. We went down to Australia in Sydney 20-39 and then lost 7-40 to the All Blacks at the Westpac Stadium in Wellington. The entire Bok squad then relocated to Durban to prepare for our first home game against the Wallabies. It was a massive Test for us in the bigger scheme of things. It was going to be the first time the full-strength side would play together in a long time and the guys were up for it. The mood in the camp was good and for me it was a very big occasion, playing my first big Test back for the Springboks in Durban, at Kings Park, where it had all started for me almost 10 years previously. We had our training sessions at Northwood High School and were based in Umhlanga at the Beverly Hills Hotel. Preparations were going well; we all knew what was expected of us and we had our game plan, but also knew that we could play what was in front of us.

The build-up to the Test was huge. You could sense that there was immense expectation for us to lay down a marker. These two fixtures (against the Wallabies and the All Blacks) were important to build some momentum for the World Cup and we were determined to play for each other and show 100% commitment. We came out really pumped up. We dominated the early passages of play but the rustiness of not having played together for a while caused us to miss out on converting some scoring chances – and at Test level the margin is so thin, that if you don't nail down the opportunities when they come, you pay for it. We were very good at times in the first half but just couldn't find the synergy to capitalise on several good build-ups. I slotted a penalty but then missed one I should have nailed in spite of the heavy wind swirling around the stadium. The ball was blown over twice and Heinrich Brüssow had to hold the ball steady while I attempted the kick. I also missed a drop-goal attempt, but felt that my distribution and defence was fine. At the same time, I felt the effects of not having had game time in the past few weeks.

We led by 6-0 but it should have been by more and we paid the price early in the second half for not converting pressure into points. We were penalised for a few infringements and the Wallabies started to get their tails up. We ended up losing the game 9-14, but we felt we had not done badly and knew that match fitness and synergy would come from playing matches. We were confident we'd post a better result the following week against the All Blacks in Port Elizabeth.

It was extremely disappointing not to have beaten the Wallabies but it certainly wasn't all doom and gloom. We'd been through the same thing in 2007. It was like a replay, and we were geared towards setting things straight and getting one over the All Blacks before going to the World Cup. Although I felt reasonably fit, I knew that I'd lacked game time in the past few weeks, so I needed that next 80 minutes to get more settled. But then something happened – I was dropped for Morné Steyn. Peter came to me at breakfast on the Monday and said he was going to give my legs a break and give Morné a run. Give my legs a break? I hadn't played for nearly two months and was as fresh as a daisy. I don't mind being dropped but just tell me I'm dropped. I chatted to Dick Muir, who mentioned that Percy Montgomery had said in their meetings that a kick was going to win us the World Cup. So I think missing that kick in Durbs had been my downfall!

Needless to say, Morné turned in a very sound game, single-handedly kicking the Boks to victory, and really grabbed his chance with both hands.

14

OLD BILL COMES KNOCKING AGAIN

I t was really important that we beat the All Blacks. There was incredible pressure on the squad to win because of the defeat against Australia in Durban. The management had made it clear that the priority was the World Cup and by sending a youthful and inexperienced side to Australia and New Zealand for the away leg of the Tri-Nations, it meant there was always the risk of us having to get bonus-point wins in both matches at home to win the trophy. I don't have to tell you how difficult that is against the Wallabies and All Blacks, so when we lost you can imagine the stress it put on all of us to get a result in Port Elizabeth.

Every Test match is important and no guy I have ever played with accepts he is going to be coming second, but we also appreciated the methodology of the management and everyone bought into the fact that winning the Tri-Nations would be secondary to winning the World Cup. Of course we wanted to do well in the Tri-Nations, but the turnaround time was less than a month between our final Tri-Nations match and the World Cup opener against Wales, which we felt would determine who would play Ireland in the World Cup quarter-finals. At least that is what we all expected because the Australians were definitely the favourites to beat Ireland in their pool match in Auckland.

The South African public and media are not forgiving at all and want success every time the Boks play, and I can understand that. We really believed we could beat Australia in Durban even though many of the match 22 had not played for more than a month. We'd trained really well in Rustenburg and bonded as a unit. There was good energy in the squad, but that had to be translated into at least one victory, hopefully two. When we lost against the Wallabies, losing the following week to the All Blacks was something every player refused to accept could happen. We owed it to ourselves, the management and South Africa to leave for the World Cup with at least one victory, and they don't come harder or sweeter than against the All Blacks. Individual aspirations and individual egos would not be tolerated and while I wanted to be starting at flyhalf I accepted the coach's decision of who should play.

The win gave us a massive boost as players. We were confident, as a squad, that we could beat the All Blacks, but there is no denying we took a blow in losing at home to the Wallabies. Bok teams shouldn't lose at home to anyone. We had beaten the All Blacks and weren't interested in them being described as a second-choice All Blacks side. When you play any of New Zealand's five Super Rugby franchises it is bloody tough, and we had won a Test against New Zealand. That's always reason to have a beer and a celebration. We felt good about ourselves and we felt confident about our World Cup campaign. We backed ourselves as individuals and as a unit. Many of the squad had experienced winning the World Cup in 2007 and there was a natural confidence in our ability to do it again. There was never arrogance, but there was belief we were good enough to beat anyone.

I was incredibly excited at the opportunity to be part of a World Cup tournament again. I felt pretty low when I missed out in 2003, as I felt I had a good chance of making the squad, and when I went to the 2007 World Cup in France I never thought of it as being my last chance as a World Cup player. I was young enough to make another tournament if my form was good enough and if I stayed fit. This time was different and while much of the pre-tournament ritual was consistent with what I had experienced in 2007 there was a vast difference in the degree of emotion.

After the Port Elizabeth win against the All Blacks, we completed our World Cup preparation in Joburg. Our team building was special and it will always be a career highlight. The management had not given any indication of what it would be, other than to let us know we'd be inspired. It started brilliantly when Lewis Pugh visited the squad. Lewis is known as the 'Human Polar Bear' for setting all sorts of swimming records in the most extreme conditions, especially in the Arctic, and I found his talk particularly inspiring. He illustrated how strong the mind can be but also how unbreakable the human spirit is if there is always hope and belief.

We were all buzzing after Lewis' visit and the excitement got greater when we took a bus to the airport. No one knew we'd be flying to the Kruger Park and the only thing that dulled my excitement was the fear of having to fly in those small planes. The management divided us into four groups, with each group representing the colour of our pool opposition at the World Cup. Each group was led on a trail, which eventually ended up at a base camp. Each group had about an hour's walk to reach the camp, during which time there would be discussion about the qualities and vulnerability of that particular team and how each player felt we could and would beat them. The idea was to get every player's contribution and later that evening the respective groups would share their views.

The most incredible thing was there had been a lion kill on a buffalo not far from our base camp. Our talking had scared away the lions and all we saw was the buffalo carcass. Our ranger made sure we were in the enclosed area of the camp, which was bordered by an electric fence, and then dragged the carcass to within 100 metres of where we would be having a few beers. He said the carcass could attract lions and hyena and it could make for interesting viewing.

Initially nothing happened and we got on with our team building. The management had invited Gary Kirsten to share his experience of coaching India to the Cricket World Cup win in India in 2011. Gary played for the Proteas as an opening batsman but his greatest success was coaching India to the No 1 ranking in Test cricket and winning the World Cup. It was the first time in 28 years that India had triumphed in a World Cup and Gary spoke to us about the pressures of managing the expectation of the fanatical and passionate support base. He hadn't been speaking for long when we could hardly hear him because several lions and hyena had returned to the buffalo carcass. The noise was so loud as the animals sorted each other out and enjoyed their feed that Gary had no option but to stop talking. Everyone just sat in silence listening to the feast going on 100 metres away. Fortunately we didn't have to wait too long before Gary got to finish his speech.

It was amazing what he had gone through as a foreign coach in India and also the extent of the pressure on Indian players to succeed every time the national cricket side plays. He spoke about how they embraced the pressure, instead of trying to run from it and turned it all into positive energy. The talks by Lewis and Gary were very different but both struck at the core of what was needed to be the first team to defend rugby's World Cup.

The Afrikaans singer Robbie Wessels is quite a favourite among many of the players and there he was (along with his *boet*) performing at the campside fire for the guys. The players were really relaxed and as the beer consumption increased so did the possibility of a few blokes getting up to no good, if all in the name of a laugh. It was quite late when we heard something in the bush, on the outskirts of the camp. The ranger shone his spotlight and there was Bismarck du Plessis, Frans Steyn and Heinrich Brüssow leopard crawling through the bush ... the ranger was not impressed when the guys told him they were trying to stalk the lions. He quickly told John Smit to get them back inside the camp. The boys were having a bit of fun but it would not have been a laughing matter if something had happened. Imagine the media headlines: 'Boks Mauled By Lions' ... I joke about it now, but we could see the ranger wasn't joking at all!

The 2011 World Cup squad announcement was aired live on SuperSport and will always be remembered for South African singer Ard Matthews infamously butchering our national anthem. I got the giggles long before Ard's shocker and somehow couldn't stop laughing. It wasn't that I didn't appreciate the occasion or meant to show disrespect to anyone, but I started laughing during the ceremony and couldn't contain myself. You know when you start laughing because you're not allowed to be laughing in the first place? It started with the capping ceremony that preceded the singing of the anthem. My mate Gregg Fry asked me to raise my eyebrow as an acknowledgement to him when I sat down after being presented with my cap. It was more an instruction (as mates do) than a request. When I sat down after being presented with my cap I had done as 'instructed', but the problem was that as I raised my eyebrow I saw myself on the playback television monitor. It looked so funny that I chuckled and then started laughing a bit louder. I knew I had to be serious which made it even worse. Some of the other guys around me started laughing as well and it was all on. Then Ard started butchering the anthem. Put yourself in that position. I am like a naughty boy at church who starts laughing when everyone is silent, and then the minister cocks up his sermon while I am trying to control the laughter.

The send-off we got before we left was mind-blowing. I thought I had experienced just about everything when we toured the country in 2007 after winning the World Cup, but the support, enthusiasm and passion from our fans was a new experience. Thousands had gone to Nelson Mandela Square in Sandton to greet us and there were thousands more at Oliver Tambo International Airport. Wow!

We were based in Wellington for the first fortnight of the tournament for our matches against Wales and Fiji and the reception in Wellington was low key, but for the first of many haka. It felt weird being in Wellington when the World Cup buzz seemed to be in Auckland from what we were seeing on TV.

There was healthy respect for Wales. They had beaten England and Argentina in World Cup warm-up matches and they were a settled combination. They were a young side that had come close to beating us in Cardiff in 2010. We were taking nothing for granted. I knew I would not be starting against Wales. Morné Steyn had started against the All Blacks and kicked 18 points. There was an emphasis on the need for a goal-kicker of his quality and it bugged me that there was doubt I could deliver as a goal-kicker. I had kicked two from three against Australia in Durban and the one that I missed probably cost me my starting place at flyhalf in the World Cup. We were leading 6-0 in that match and as I was about to kick the wind blew over the ball. Everything went wrong with the kick after that. It was rushed and it wasn't ideal that the ball had to be kept on the tee by the finger of a player because of the wind. I am not excusing the miss, but trying to put it into context.

Wellington, as a city, is notorious for strong winds and the Westpac Stadium is one of the more difficult for goal-kickers. We beat Wales 17-16 after trailing 10-16 with 20 minutes to go. I played the last hour as a centre replacement for Jean de Villiers, but could never do as good a job. He is world class and one of the best international No 12s. I have never been keen on playing No 12. As with any Bok you play where the coach wants you, but my position has always been No 10. I feel comfortable there and in control. I never doubt myself as a flyhalf but I am not confident at centre, and I never have been.

It was great to be part of the win, but we didn't know that night that beating Wales would mean us playing Australia in the quarter-finals. With no disrespect to Ireland, who have beaten the Boks a couple of times in the past decade, we expected Australia to beat Ireland, which would mean we played Ireland in the quarter-finals. We obviously had to win all our matches to finish first but we never doubted our capacity to do so.

Our training schedule in the early part of the tournament was intense and I had worked on my goal-kicking because of the possibility that it could come down to a penalty kick from me to win us the World Cup. I overdid it and the load was too much. It was out of sync with how I had ever prepared and my groin tightened up at training early in the second week of the tournament. It ruled me out of the Fiji match, which we won 49-3, but Peter de Villiers had told me I would be starting against Namibia.

It proved to be a low point of my tournament. I couldn't train, I couldn't even find some comfort in a game of golf because of the nature of the injury and I felt pretty useless.

I spent a lot of time in my room, which is never a good thing, and the only day I remember smiling in the week of the Fiji Test was when my old mate Bob Skinstad (former Bok captain and now SuperSport analyst) took me for lunch.

When we got to Taupo to prepare for the Namibia match the injury had not healed. I still couldn't train and I could feel my World Cup slipping away. I wanted so badly to make a contribution. I'd won a World Cup with a great bunch of players in 2007 and I'd played an intense 2007 World Cup campaign without injury. It was getting to me big time that I couldn't train. I wanted to push through the pain and make myself available but I knew that I would only make it worse. The groin had improved but it was when kicking that I could feel the strain and the tightening. I was desperate to play, but I knew I would be doing no one any good. The boys thumped Namibia 87-0 and even though it was a Springbok World Cup record win there wasn't any over-the-top celebration. We knew Samoa would be a reminder of what was needed to progress beyond the quarter-finals.

Management gave the players a couple days off and Jean arranged a kombi for us to take a road trip from Auckland to Lake Taupo. The drive time is around three hours; it took us nine. Pierre Spies, who doesn't drink much by way of booze, was our designated driver. We stopped at every little town on the way for a top up and a release. It was a necessary unwind before the battle against the Samoans, who were being talked up as a real threat to knock us over. The trip was good for everyone and my spirits were lifted when I made it through the Monday training session. I felt a bit stiff but there was no more strain. I told the medical staff I was good to go and they said if I wasn't I was being sent home. I declared myself fit for selection but Peter said he was going with Morné at flyhalf and Frans at inside centre.

I was gutted not to play Samoa. I really thought my style of play at No 10 and the physical nature of my game was

Above (clockwise from top left): Getting a good hit on Sam Tuitupou for Bath in 2008; after my last game at The Rec, with my mates Pieter Dixon and Michael Claassens; on the way to the tryline to score against Leicester in 2008; the try meant a lot to me, one of my best moments in a Bath shirt
Below: The Rec during a night game. Such an awesome atmosphere

Opposite page: (clockwise from top left): With Jean de Villiers and BJ Botha at the 2010 Laureus World Sports Awards in Abu Dhabi; Jean and me, about to get into a DTM touring car; at the Sport for Good Football Tournament at Emirates Palace Hotel in 2010; meeting up with the boys in London while I was at Bath and they were on tour; Julia and me on a boat cruise during our honeymoon in the Maldives
This page (top to bottom): With Michael after Bath won the European Challenge Cup final in 2008; celebrating with the boys in the change room after the game; at a Bath Christmas party, which had a 'Las Vegas' theme. Check out Elvis!

Opposite page: Playing for the Lions during the 2011 Super Rugby competition. Local businessmen Ivor Ichikowitz and Robert Gumede *(top left)* were pivotal in bringing me to Joburg

This page (clockwise from top left): Facing up to Australia in the 2008 Tri-Nations at Kings Park; our Test against Argentina at Ellis Park; introducing myself to Dan Carter at the Westpac Stadium in Wellington in 2008; at a Springbok practice in 2010

Opposite page (clockwise from top left): Running drills at Rugby League Park in Wellington during the 2011 Rugby World Cup; our itinerary for the day of our 2011 World Cup quarter-final against Australia; with camera in hand during the Boks' trip to Huka Falls, in Taupo, New Zealand; limbering up during a training session in Taupo

This page (clockwise from top): Getting vertical against the Aussies at Kings Park in the 2011 Tri-Nations; fooling around with Bok prankster Jaque Fourie; with President Jacob Zuma at the Presidential Guest House before the Boks' departure to the 2011 Rugby World Cup; signing autographs at the Museum of New Zealand in Wellington; attempting a drop against Australia in our game at Kings Park in 2011

SPRINGBOK

SPRINGBOK MATCH DAY PROGRAMME
RWC 2011 Quarter Final
9 October 2011
Wellington

SUNDAY
9 October 2011

Time	Activity	Location
08:00 – 10:00	Breakfast	Amora Chambers
09:30 – 10:30	Preparation of Change Rooms	Wellington Regional Stadium
13:15 – 13:30	Stretching	Amora Chambers
13:30 – 14:00	Pre-Match Meal	Amora Chambers
14:30 – 16:00	Strapping	Physiotherapy Room
15:30	Logistics depart to Westpac Stadium	
16:00 – 16:15	Top-Up Meal	Amora Chambers
16:15	Non-Playing Reserves and Management take their seats on the Bus	

Attire to Stadium: Match 22 and On-Field Support Staff (Presentation Track Suit, White Polyester Golf-Shirt, Navy Rain Jacket for on-field support staff); Head Coach, Assistant Coaches, Non-Playing Reserves and other Officials (Green Blazer, Black Pants, Black Shoes, White Shirt, Black Belt, Black Socks, Springbok Tie, Sleeveless Green Jersey or White Jersey, Black Coat optional)

Time	Activity	Location
16:15 – 16:21	Team Talk	Amora Chambers
	Match 22 and Coaches	
16:23	Bus depart to Westpac Stadium	
16:30	Bus arrives at Westpac Stadium	
16:32	Confirmation of Team and Submission of Match Team Sheet	
16:40 – 16:43	On-field flash Interview with the Coach	
16:40 – 17:15	Additional Strapping	
16:45 – 16:50	Clothing and Equipment Check, Match Officials Briefing and Front Row Instructions	
17:10 – 17:20	Elastic Band Warm-up	
17:15	Kickers Out	
17:20	Coin Toss	
	Decision regarding Kick-off or Receive and Running Direction can be immediate or latest by 17:30	
17:22 – 17:42	Warm-up Drills	
17:30	Radio Check	
17:45	Field of Play to be Cleared	
17:45	Coaches to their Box	
17:15	Countdown to Run On	
17:53:30	Springboks leave the Change Rooms	
	Presentation Track Suit Bottoms	
17:54:20	Teams Assemble at Mouth of the Tunnel	
	Future Captains meet Captains prior to entry to Field of Play	
17:55:05	Flag Bearers lead Teams out to the Field of Play	
17:56:35	South African National Anthem	
18:01:30 – 18:43	**South Africa versus Australia 1st Half**	
18:43 – 18:55	Half Time	
18:55 – 19:40	**South Africa versus Australia 2nd Half**	
19:40 – 19:45	On-field flash interview with Captain for Sky NZ	
19:45 – 19:50	In-tunnel unilateral interview with Captain for SuperSport	
19:50 – 19:55	In-tunnel unilateral interview with Head Coach for Sky NZ and SuperSport	
19:50 – 20:30	Recovery (individual 10 minute massage)	
19:58 – 20:00	Man of the match in-tunnel interview for Sky NZ and SuperSport	
20:10 – 20:25	In-tunnel unilaterals with at least four RWC-nominated players for SuperSport and general rights holders	
20:30 – 20:45	Post-Match Media Conference	
	Coach and Captain	
20:50 – 21:20	Mixed Zone for minimum ten personnel including two coaches and captain	
	Springbok Bus depart to Intercontinental Hotel after conclusion of Mixed Zone	
	Players assemble in Team Room on arrival	
	Team Meeting	Amora Chambers
	Dinner	Amora Chambers

Above, middle and below right: In action during our pool game against Wales at the 2011 Rugby World Cup
Below left: Watching our quarter-final match unfold against Australia, with John Smit and Bryan Habana

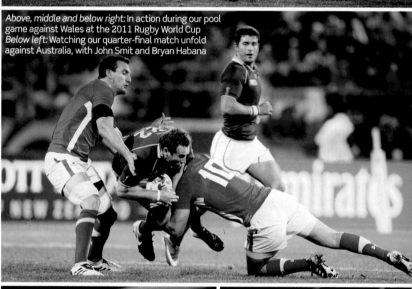

ideal to negate the Samoans, but it didn't help that there was doubt over my groin. The coaches went with a five forwards and two backs bench split and I couldn't realistically expect to be on the bench. I don't offer that kind of versatility. My wife Julia arrived before the game, which made up for the disappointment of not playing, but the truth is that it isn't the greatest feeling being at a World Cup and not being involved in the match 22. You have to work hard to make sure you remain positive but it is easier said than done.

I knew it would be tough and that there wasn't going to be a lot in the result. We all did. We also knew how physical the game would be but I don't think any of us expected so much off-the-ball play. The last 20 minutes was frantic. They threw everything at us. It was hard but it also got quite dirty. Welsh referee Nigel Owens lost a bit of control in that period and there was plenty going on off the ball. Our discipline was outstanding and Smitty's yellow card for a professional foul was ridiculous. I don't think Smitty could believe he nearly got the intercept, let alone have a premeditated plan to knock down the pass.

I felt very frustrated watching the game and I wasn't impressed with the way the Samoans conducted themselves on the field, and even more so off the field. A lot was being said after the match that Owens favoured us. I thought he made some poor calls against Samoa but I felt we got the worst of the calls. As I have already said, I think he lost control of the game in that last quarter. I have always had respect for how the Samoans play the game and especially for how they interact after the contest. All the bitching and bad blood after this one meant I lost a lot of respect for those particular Samoan players.

The match was played on a Friday evening on Auckland's North Shore at the North Harbour Stadium and we spent the rest of the weekend in Auckland. It meant we could get in some golf and on the Sunday Jean and I got our first win against Schalla (Schalk Burger) and Smitty. It had been a long time coming.

The Samoan game proved costly to the team with Frans ruled out of the World Cup because of a shoulder injury. There was also some doubt over whether Francois Hougaard would play in the quarter-final because he took a knock to the head against Samoa. Hougie didn't know where he was or what had happened, and the guys, while concerned, also seized on the chance to take the piss out of him. He kept on asking what had happened and was clearly a little bit out of it, so when we got back to the change room Bakkies Botha said to him: 'Hey, you must hurry and go shower, your wife's waiting for you …' I added: 'Ja Hougie, hurry, your wife and kids are waiting. You must hurry!' He seemed very confused and correctly so. Hougie isn't married and doesn't have kids. We all had a laugh watching him after his shower. He seemed unsure he had showered, so we reminded him that he needed to. He kept on fiddling with his hair to see if he had in fact showered. He was totally confused! The final straw was when he asked about the final score. We said 53-2. It took him a while to realise one team can't get just two points in a game. I am sure that if it wasn't a World Cup quarter-final the next weekend he would have been out for a few weeks, but he was desperate to play Australia.

We were back in Wellington where it had all started for us in the 2011 World Cup. The Welsh win seemed years away. There was a different energy to that first week. This was do or die. We knew if we lost we were gone. The tournament rules state you have 24 hours to get out the country, and we didn't want to be going home just yet. We believed we could create history and become the first team to defend the World Cup. We had injury setbacks but we backed the strength of the players in the squad to beat anyone.

Losing Frans was big because there isn't another player in the game who can kick the ball as far and bang over 60m penalties with such ease. Our week started with terrible weather and emotional send-offs to Frans and Bakkies, who was also ruled out of the tournament. Bakkies was pretty cut up because he knew he'd never again play in a Bok team with his big mate Victor Matfield. They had been the dominant lock combination in world rugby for the past five to six years and they'd won every medal there is to win for a southern hemisphere player. Victor had confirmed he would retire after the World Cup and Bakkies was off to Toulon. It was a shitty way to start the week.

Every team was being cursed with injuries. If our big one was Frans, then the biggest of the tournament was New Zealand losing Dan Carter, who tore his groin muscle kicking at posts. He had no history of groin injuries and he is the leading point-scorer in Test history. His groin went with one kick at training, in a World Cup competition, in New Zealand. I really felt for him. I've been there so often with injury, but I know that for any player, being involved in a World Cup in your own country is as big as it gets. He would never again get a chance to play in, and win, a World Cup in his own country. He was devastated and so was every New Zealander. The New Zealand media went nuts and questioned whether the All Blacks could win without him. I thought they were selling their team short. Dan's a great player, but there are some fine players in the All Blacks side and we knew that to win the World Cup we'd have to beat them in New Zealand. We had managed it in 2008 and 2009, so we knew it was possible, but before we could think of New Zealand we had to get past Australia.

I've been involved in a winning World Cup campaign, in Tri-Nations must-win matches, in Currie Cup and Super Rugby play-offs, and there is nothing that prepares you for the business end of the tournament. You have to have been there before and that is where we felt we had an edge. So many of the squad had played on the biggest stage, in Paris in 2007, and won. So many had won big finals against the best players in the world. We really felt equipped for the job.

We had field sessions that week at the Hutt Recreation Ground, which is near Petone, about 15km from the city, as well as a few video sessions. Things went well in our preparations and you could feel the intensity click up a few gears. The players seemed to be handling the pressure well. There was a steady build-up of South African support in the city and it was only near the end of the week that it intensified – my dad and father-in-law (the two Mikes) had also arrived. The one thing about a World Cup in New Zealand is that visitors attend the matches in the cities and then take road trips in the week and go back for the matches. It is a beautiful country in which to travel and the people are among the most hospitable, but there are few pleasantries on the rugby field. You earn your wins in New Zealand, even when you are not playing New Zealanders, as we found out against Wales and Samoa.

The Wallabies had beaten the Boks five times out of the last six we had played and the media was not letting us forget the statistic. The Australians had beaten the Boks 39-41 in Bloemfontein in 2010 when Kurtley Beale kicked a 50m penalty and they had knocked us over 9-14 in Durban in the 2011 Tri-Nations. Some were asking if we couldn't beat them in South Africa how could we beat them in New Zealand? We weren't asking those questions. We knew they would be difficult to beat and we certainly weren't thinking a week ahead to the All Blacks in Auckland. We were up for the challenge. We were the world champions, in New Zealand, defending a title so many of the squad had won in Paris in 2007. It was going to take a very good team to beat us, or some pretty bad luck to go against us. We had known adversity and we were embracing the pressure of expectation. We wanted to win for ourselves and for each other and for South Africa. The commitment and belief was never questioned. We also knew that if we lost this game it would be the end for so many of us who had been in Paris on 20 October 2007.

Match day is always inspiring in smaller cities where you get to sense the excitement and can interact with the people. Our bus trip to the stadium from the Amora Hotel was a short one but an emotional one. It is fantastic to see so many Bok supporters, to hear the chants of 'Bokke!' and to see the expectation on every supporter's face. We embraced it. We wanted to deliver for everyone. I wasn't starting but was included in the match 22 and I was as pumped for the match as I was for the 2007 World Cup final in Paris. My role was very different now. Four years ago I was the No 10 and the go-to guy. Peter had gone with Morné as his No 10 and I had to support the decision. This wasn't about who wore what number or who played where. It was about the Boks beating Australia and getting to Auckland a week later to play the All Blacks in a World Cup semi-final.

Our boys played with such intensity, controlled all the early play and through one turnover and one penalty were 8-0 down. It was never a reflection of the play and that is why there was no panic on our side. We continued to build our game and trust our ability to break down their defence and deny them the continuity they so thrive on. Give Australians ball to build phases and their backs will bury you. Deny them this fluidity and they are very vulnerable. Everything went to plan except the end result.

We lost Heinrich early which meant Australia's openside specialist David Pocock would be even more of a presence at the breakdown, but we were dominant everywhere. The longer the game went the more it looked like the dam wall, which was Australia's defensive line, was going to burst. They had been organised and brave in defence but our attack was relentless. We had plenty ball and all the control. We also had all the field position. We should have scored but spilt the ball a few times and I don't think we were helped by the referee Bryce Lawrence's interpretations. But I never doubted we could win and when Morné kicked a trademark drop goal to give us a 9-8 lead with 20 minutes to go I felt we would put them away.

Sitting on the bench, as I have said, is awful because you are involved but you are as removed as the guy sitting in the worst seat in the stand. You are powerless to do anything. The game seemed to go on for an eternity when we had the lead, but when James O'Connor kicked the penalty to take them ahead 11-9 with five minutes to go it seemed like it was over in a blink. I thought Australia's defence was as good as I've seen, but we found holes and we created opportunities. Nothing went for us. Two passes were ruled forward. That was two tries. Twice we were over their line and we lost the ball. We were so dominant. For the record, we were forced to make just 53 tackles against the Wallabies' 147, we stole five of their lineout throws without conceding one, we had 56% possession and enjoyed 76% territory. Translating that on the scoreboard was the one thing we didn't do. It was just so bizarre. I couldn't believe it. The end whistle blew. We were gone. We were no longer world champions. I felt sick and I couldn't change anything.

That night the journey ended for so many of us who had been involved with the Springboks for so long. Our final fines meeting, which we call the kontiki, was incredibly emotional. This group of Bok players and management are amazing people and we had been through so much as a unit. I had low points at the tournament but that never detracted from appreciating the environment. That was highlighted afterwards in the change room. I don't think there was a person who didn't shed a tear. We all had a chance to stand up and say something. It was really the most emotional I've ever seen a Bok change room after a game and I've witnessed them in various moods over the past 10 years. We not only said goodbye to the Webb Ellis Cup but also said goodbye to some legends of Springbok rugby that night.

15

EVERY PICTURE TELLS A STORY

I am not a big reader of books so being sent the final edits of my own book meant more reading than I've done since my school days, and somehow I initially even found a way around that.

I must confess I got my wife Julia to read me the first eight draft chapters as bedtime stories, and I managed to stay awake, but once at the World Cup, I didn't have that luxury and it was down to me to do the final proof in terms of the accuracy of what I had said. It is something that has surprised my mates (me actually reading) because it's pretty well known I'll take a movie over a book.

Mathew Cairns (better known as Faff) is a mate of mine who used to go to Maritzburg College but moved with his family to New Zealand in the mid-90s. I caught up with him during the World Cup and told him about the book. He was quick to remind me about an interview I did many years ago. I was asked if I liked reading and I obviously said 'not really'. The guy doing the interview persisted and wanted to know what my favourite books were so I said the ones with the pictures in them, so the fun part of the book was … yup … deciding which pictures go where!

The book's deadline was the weekend of the World Cup final, as we had envisaged the Boks being in the final at Eden Park and there being a Maritzburg College old boy in the Bok mix. Well I didn't get there and neither did the Boks, but one College old boy who did is referee Craig Joubert. Fellow South African Jonathan Kaplan or England's Wayne Barnes were expected by many to blow the World Cup final, but Craig was so impressive during the All Blacks' 20-6 semi-final win against the Wallabies that he got the nod. I thought he did a great job in the decider considering the enormity of the occasion. Some say he could have awarded France a penalty when they took the ball through 16 phases near the end, but there were no clear transgressions and I'm sure Craig didn't want the winners to be determined by a dodgy penalty. In the end, the All Blacks claimed an 8-7 victory to become deserved world champions.

Craig has just turned 33 and I am glad his youthfulness, at least when it comes to referees, did not count against him being rewarded with the biggest game of his life. He deserved the recognition and is massively respected by the players. He is also a good bloke, which isn't something I'd say about every referee I've met over the past decade.

I played in the Currie Cup semi-finals for the Lions that weekend and the only thing I'd have traded it for was the chance to be at Eden Park playing in a World Cup final. I am committed to another season with the Lions in Super Rugby in 2012 and having spent the last month with the squad in the 2011 campaign I got an insight into players I'd never met before. I can tell you that talk of the Lions making the 2012 Super Rugby play-offs isn't the mad talk it may have been a few years ago. John Mitchell is a very good coach and there are talented individuals in the squad – quite a few of whom are good enough to play for the Boks.

I want to win a Currie Cup and Super Rugby title in 2012 and make a contribution to passing on whatever rugby knowledge I have to the younger generation, but I can't say with certainty what I want to do when I finish playing. I know I will have an involvement in some capacity, but I also know I will take a little time away from the game when the knees do finally go.

All I've ever known, as an adult, is rugby and it has taken me around the world a few times to some of the most amazing places, the odd depressing one and more than a few interesting ones. Mostly it has introduced me to a lot of wonderful people.

I've experienced everything from the emotional low of defeat, injury, and operations, to the amazing high of winning a World Cup as the Springbok flyhalf. All of the knocks can't beat that night in Paris on 20 October 2007. That remains the most memorable of my rugby life. It made every injury and operation seem worthwhile.

Rugby is in my blood and I'll never want to deny that. I quite fancy the idea of being a defence and skills coach somewhere, but I do first want to enjoy just being back in South Africa.

As previously mentioned, I have a stake in an ad agency, Sugar, in Durban and because I am currently at the Lions and living in Joburg it may be that we'll set up a satellite office in this city. Hey, I may even get to look after one or two accounts. Maybe I'll take my golf more seriously and play professionally … or you may just find me playing on the flank for College Rovers!

Who knows what's around the next bend? The initial plan is to get back to Durban in the next year or two and start a family. I know Julia would appreciate just being in one place and having me with her. She's been all over the world with me and I know it isn't the easiest of lives being married to a professional rugby player. The tours are always harder on the one back home, having to look after everything. I will never be able to thank her enough for the sacrifice and for encouraging and allowing me to be Butch.

As you would have figured if you've read this far I'm a chilled guy when not making a tackle and my mates felt it pertinent I give you an insight into the basic essentials of my likes:

My favourite food is lamb.

My favourite colour is white.

My favourite music is rock.

My favourite movie is *Old School.*

My favourite car is a Ferrari F430.

My sports hero is Ernie Els.

My rugby hero is James Small.

My favourite clothing brands are Nike and Diesel.

My favourite pastime is having knee ops.

And my biggest fear is retiring.

The thing I will miss most about rugby are the friends you make and the good times you have with those friends.

The thing I will least miss about rugby is pre–season fitness training.

The thing I look forward to most when I don't play rugby anymore is having my weekends to myself to do anything I want.

I have no superstitions or rituals before a game.

I do love tackling, but then I didn't have to tell you that.

Enjoy the pictures.

CAREER STATISTICS

KEY

F = Final	R = Replacement

SPRINGBOKS (TESTS)

Date	Opponents	Position	T	C	P	D	Pts	Result	Score*
16/06/2001	France	Flyhalf						Lost	23-32
23/06/2001	France	Flyhalf			5		15	Won	20-15
21/07/2001	New Zealand	Flyhalf						Lost	3-12
28/07/2001	Australia	Flyhalf						Won	20-15
18/08/2001	Australia	Flyhalf						Drew	14-14
25/08/2001	New Zealand	Flyhalf						Lost	15-26
09/11/2002	France	Fullback (R)						Lost	10-30
16/11/2002	Scotland	Flyhalf			2		6	Lost	6-21
23/11/2002	England	Centre						Lost	3-53
22/07/2006	New Zealand	Flyhalf						Lost	17-35
05/08/2006	Australia	Flyhalf		1	2		8	Lost	18-20
26/08/2006	New Zealand	Flyhalf			1		3	Lost	26-45
02/09/2006	New Zealand	Centre (R)						Won	21-20
18/11/2006	England	Flyhalf	1	1	2		13	Lost	21-23
26/05/2007	England	Flyhalf						Won	58-10
02/06/2007	England	Flyhalf		1			2	Won	55-22
16/06/2007	Australia	Flyhalf						Won	22-19
23/06/2007	New Zealand	Flyhalf	1				5	Lost	21-26
15/08/2007	Namibia	Flyhalf						Won	105-13
25/08/2007	Scotland	Flyhalf						Won	27-3
09/09/2007	Samoa	Flyhalf						Won	59-7

SPRINGBOKS (TESTS) *(continued)*

Date	Opponents	Position	T	C	P	D	Pts	Result	Score*
14/09/2007	England	Flyhalf						Won	36-0
30/09/2007	USA	Flyhalf		2			4	Won	64-15
07/10/2007	Fiji	Flyhalf	1				5	Won	37-20
14/10/2007	Argentina	Flyhalf						Won	37-13
20/10/2007	England	Flyhalf						Won	15-6
07/06/2008	Wales	Flyhalf		4	5		23	Won	43-17
14/06/2008	Wales	Flyhalf		4	3		17	Won	37-21
05/07/2008	New Zealand	Flyhalf			1		3	Lost	8-19
12/07/2008	New Zealand	Flyhalf			2	1	9	Won	30-28
19/07/2008	Australia	Flyhalf			1		3	Lost	9-16
09/08/2008	Argentina	Flyhalf		9			18	Won	63-9
16/08/2008	New Zealand	Flyhalf						Lost	0-19
23/08/2008	Australia	Flyhalf			1		3	Lost	15-27
30/08/2008	Australia	Flyhalf		3	1		9	Won	53-8
19/06/2010	Italy	Centre						Won	29-13
26/06/2010	Italy	Flyhalf (R)						Won	55-11
10/07/2010	New Zealand	Flyhalf (R)						Lost	12-32
24/07/2010	Australia	Flyhalf (R)						Lost	13-30
28/08/2010	Australia	Flyhalf (R)		1			2	Won	44-31
13/08/2011	Australia	Flyhalf			2		6	Lost	9-14
11/09/2011	Wales	Centre (R)						Won	17-16
42 matches			3	26	28	1	154		
Record			P: 42; W: 23; L: 18; D: 1; Win%: 54.7						

*Springboks score first

SPRINGBOKS (NON TEST MATCHES)

Date	Opponents	Position	T	C	P	D	Pts	Result	Score*
21/08/2007	Connacht	Centre		1	1		5	Won	18-3
1 match			0	1	1	0	5		
Record			P: 1; W: 1; Win%: 100						

*Springboks score first

SHARKS (SUPER RUGBY)

Date	Opponents	Position	T	C	P	D	Pts	Result	Score*
23/02/2001	Bulls	Flyhalf		3	3		15	Won	30-17

SHARKS (SUPER RUGBY) *(continued)*									
Date	**Opponents**	**Position**	**T**	**C**	**P**	**D**	**Pts**	**Result**	**Score***
03/03/2001	Brumbies	Flyhalf			1		3	Won	17-16
10/03/2001	Highlanders	Flyhalf		1	3		11	Won	30-29
17/03/2001	Hurricanes	Flyhalf		2	5		19	Won	39-21
24/03/2001	Waratahs	Flyhalf						Won	42-17
30/03/2001	Cats	Flyhalf (R)			1	1	6	Lost	25-26
07/04/2001	Blues	Flyhalf	1	3	5		26	Won	41-27
14/04/2001	Chiefs	Flyhalf		2			4	Won	24-8
22/04/2001	Reds	Flyhalf (R)		1	1		5	Lost	27-32
28/04/2001	Crusaders	Flyhalf		3	1		9	Lost	24-34
12/05/2001	Stormers	Flyhalf		1	2		8	Won	23-19
19/05/2001	Cats	Flyhalf		1	1		5	Won	30-12
26/05/2001	Brumbies (F)	Flyhalf			2		6	Lost	6-36
21/02/2003	Stormers	Flyhalf			1		3	Lost	18-40
01/03/2003	Brumbies	Flyhalf		1	6		20	Won	25-17
08/03/2003	Waratahs	Flyhalf		4	1		11	Lost	36-49
21/03/2003	Highlanders	Flyhalf			3		9	Lost	19-23
29/03/2003	Cats	Flyhalf		3		1	9	Won	29-23
12/04/2003	Chiefs	Flyhalf		4	1		11	Won	31-25
18/04/2003	Crusaders	Flyhalf		1	1	1	8	Lost	18-23
26/04/2003	Blues	Flyhalf		1	3		11	Lost	16-25
03/05/2003	Reds	Flyhalf		1	2		8	Lost	13-22
10/05/2003	Bulls	Flyhalf		1	3		11	Lost	16-24
21/02/2004	Bulls	Centre		2	3		13	Won	23-18
28/02/2004	Waratahs	Centre		2			4	Lost	14-48
06/03/2004	Brumbies	Flyhalf			5		15	Lost	20-23
12/03/2004	Highlanders	Flyhalf	1	4	1		16	Won	36-35
19/03/2004	Hurricanes	Flyhalf		1	3		11	Won	21-20
03/04/2004	Cats	Flyhalf		4	3		17	Won	42-28
10/04/2004	Crusaders	Flyhalf		3	1		9	Won	29-25
16/04/2004	Chiefs	Flyhalf		3	2		12	Lost	27-34
24/04/2004	Reds	Flyhalf						Lost	5-6
30/04/2004	Blues	Flyhalf	1	2	4		21	Lost	26-37
08/05/2004	Stormers	Flyhalf						Lost	24-31
25/02/2005	Stormers	Flyhalf	1	1			7	Lost	12-26
05/03/2005	Waratahs	Flyhalf		1	2		8	Lost	13-36

SHARKS (SUPER RUGBY) *(continued)*

Date	Opponents	Position	T	C	P	D	Pts	Result	Score*
11/03/2005	Hurricanes	Centre		2	2		10	Lost	23-29
26/03/2005	Brumbies	Flyhalf						Won	36-24
09/04/2005	Chiefs	Flyhalf						Lost	5-40
07/05/2005	Bulls	Flyhalf		2	1		7	Lost	17-23
06/05/2006	Stormers	Flyhalf						Won	24-17
12/05/2006	Force	Flyhalf						Won	41-25
03/02/2007	Bulls	Flyhalf						Won	17-3
09/02/2007	Waratahs	Flyhalf	1				5	Won	22-9
17/02/2007	Highlanders	Centre (R)						Won	23-16
03/03/2007	Crusaders	Flyhalf						Won	27-26
10/03/2007	Cheetahs	Flyhalf						Won	30-14
17/03/2007	Hurricanes	Flyhalf		2	1		7	Won	27-14
24/03/2007	Brumbies	Flyhalf		1			2	Lost	10-21
30/03/2007	Force	Flyhalf						Lost	12-22
07/04/2007	Reds	Flyhalf						Won	59-16
14/04/2007	Blues	Fullback (R)						Won	32-25
21/04/2007	Chiefs	Wing (R)						Lost	27-35
28/04/2007	Lions	Flyhalf						Won	33-3
05/05/2007	Stormers	Flyhalf						Won	36-10
12/05/2007	Blues	Flyhalf	1			1	8	Won	34-18
19/05/2007	Bulls (F)	Flyhalf						Lost	19-20
57 matches			6	63	74	4	390		
Record			P: 57; W: 31; L: 26; Win%: 54.3						

*Sharks score first

LIONS (SUPER RUGBY)

Date	Opponents	Position	T	C	P	D	Pts	Result	Score*
14/05/2011	Brumbies	Centre (R)						Won	29-20
21/05/2011	Waratahs	Flyhalf						Lost	12-29
28/05/2011	Highlanders	Centre						Won	26-22
04/06/2011	Hurricanes	Centre		1			2	Lost	27-38
11/06/2011	Sharks	Flyhalf	0	3	3	0	15	Drew	30-30
5 matches			0	4	3	0	17		
Record			P: 5; W: 2; L: 2; D: 1; Win%: 40						

*Lions score first

SHARKS (CURRIE CUP)									
Date	**Opponents**	**Position**	**T**	**C**	**P**	**D**	**Pts**	**Result**	**Score***
05/06/1999	Valke	Flyhalf (R)						Won	17-12
29/07/2000	Griffons	Flyhalf						Won	46-37
04/08/2000	Boland	Flyhalf						Won	18-13
12/08/2000	E Province	Flyhalf						Won	29-15
01/09/2000	Valke	Flyhalf						Won	43-22
09/09/2000	Golden Lions	Flyhalf						Lost	35-42
16/09/2000	FS Cheetahs	Flyhalf						Won	42-12
23/09/2000	SWD	Flyhalf						Won	49-13
30/09/2000	W Province	Flyhalf						Won	28-19
06/10/2000	Pumas	Flyhalf		3			6	Won	60-27
14/10/2000	Griquas	Flyhalf						Won	35-33
21/10/2000	FS Cheetahs	Flyhalf	1				5	Won	29-15
28/10/2000	W Province (F)	Flyhalf						Lost	15-25
08/09/2001	Valke	Flyhalf (R)		1	2		8	Lost	25-30
15/09/2001	FS Cheetahs	Flyhalf		1	2		8	Lost	28-36
03/08/2002	E Province	Flyhalf (R)		2	1		7	Won	30-16
24/08/2002	Leopards	Flyhalf		6			12	Won	52-10
31/08/2002	Blue Bulls	Flyhalf		2	1		7	Drew	17-17
07/09/2002	Pumas	Flyhalf	2	4			18	Won	69-26
14/09/2002	Golden Lions	Flyhalf		4	3		17	Lost	37-46
21/09/2002	W Province	Flyhalf		2	4		16	Won	36-29
27/09/2002	FS Cheetahs	Flyhalf		2	3		13	Won	33-6
05/10/2002	Valke	Flyhalf		2	2		10	Won	44-19
12/10/2002	Griquas	Flyhalf	1	8			21	Won	78-7
19/10/2002	Blue Bulls	Flyhalf	1	1	4		19	Lost	19-22
25/07/2003	SWD	Flyhalf	1	5			15	Won	45-13
02/08/2003	Griquas	Flyhalf		4	3		17	Won	47-32
09/08/2003	Pumas	Flyhalf		3	1		9	Won	44-20
16/08/2003	W Province	Flyhalf		4	1	1	14	Won	39-34
23/08/2003	Blue Bulls	Flyhalf		3	3		15	Won	35-28
30/08/2003	Golden Lions	Flyhalf		3	4		18	Lost	38-42
06/09/2003	FS Cheetahs	Flyhalf		1	4		14	Won	24-10
13/09/2003	SWD	Flyhalf						Won	37-29
20/09/2003	Griquas	Flyhalf (R)	1	4			13	Won	48-15
27/09/2003	Pumas	Flyhalf		3	2		12	Lost	27-35

SHARKS (CURRIE CUP) (continued)

Date	Opponents	Position	T	C	P	D	Pts	Result	Score*
04/10/2003	W Province	Flyhalf			6		18	Won	18-6
11/10/2003	Blue Bulls	Flyhalf			5		15	Lost	15-20
17/10/2003	Golden Lions	Flyhalf		1			2	Lost	17-20
25/10/2003	FS Cheetahs	Flyhalf		1	2		8	Won	28-25
01/11/2003	Blue Bulls (F)	Flyhalf		2			4	Lost	19-40
23/06/2006	Golden Lions	Flyhalf		2	3		13	Won	33-22
01/07/2006	W Province	Flyhalf		2	3		13	Won	28-25
16/09/2006	Blue Bulls	Flyhalf			2		6	Lost	32-50
30/09/2006	Valke	Flyhalf (R)						Won	48-10
07/10/2006	FS Cheetahs	Flyhalf						Lost	14-30
45 matches			**7**	**76**	**61**	**1**	**373**		
Record		P: 45; W: 31; L: 13; D: 1; Win%: 68.8							

*Sharks score first

NATAL WILDEBEEST (WELSH RUGBY UNION CHALLENGE TROPHY)

Date	Opponents	Position	T	C	P	D	Pts	Result	Score*
11/01/1999	Neath	Flyhalf (R)		1			2	Won	36-18
20/01/1999	Aberavon	Flyhalf						Lost	14-20
24/01/1999	Caerphilly	Flyhalf						Won	37-32
3 matches			**0**	**1**	**0**	**0**	**2**		
Record		P: 3; W: 2; L: 1; Win%: 66							

*Natal Wildebeest score first

NATAL WILDEBEEST (VODACOM CUP)

Date	Opponents	Position	T	C	P	D	Pts	Result	Score*
05/03/1999	E Province	Flyhalf						Won	30-14
12/03/1999	Boland	Flyhalf		4			8	Won	33-12
20/03/1999	SWD	Flyhalf		1			2	Lost	7-20
26/03/1999	W Province	Flyhalf						Won	27-22
09/04/1999	FS Cheetahs	Flyhalf						Won	13-0
13/04/1999	Border	Flyhalf						Won	13-09
17/04/1999	E Province	Flyhalf						Won	27-20
24/04/1999	Boland	Flyhalf	1				5	Lost	39-47
30/04/1999	SWD	Flyhalf						Won	19-12
08/05/1999	W Province	Flyhalf	1				5	Lost	29-37

NATAL WILDEBEEST (VODACOM CUP) *(continued)*

Date	Opponents	Position	T	C	P	D	Pts	Result	Score*
22/05/1999	Young Lions	Flyhalf						Lost	3-36
04/03/2000	SWD	Flyhalf						Won	26-18
10/03/2000	W Province	Flyhalf			3		9	Won	14-13
17/03/2000	Boland	Flyhalf	2	5	1		23	Drew	38-38
25/03/2000	Border	Flyhalf		1	2		8	Lost	13-30
31/03/2000	E Province	Centre		1	2		8	Lost	18-23
08/04/2000	FS Cheetahs	Centre		2	1		7	Lost	27-37
17 matches			**4**	**14**	**9**	**0**	**75**		
Record			P: 17; W: 9; L: 7; D: 1; Win%: 53						

Natal Wildebeest score first

SOUTH AFRICA U21

Date	Opponents	Position	T	C	P	D	Pts	Result	Score*
17/07/1999	Wales	Wing (R)	1				5	Won	48-9
20/07/1999	England	Wing (R)						Won	39-5
29/05/2000	Boland XV	Centre	1				5	Won	49-29
21/06/2000	Tonga	Centre		1			2	Won	79-8
24/06/2000	Australia	Flyhalf						Won	25-24
28/06/2000	Scotland	Flyhalf						Won	38-5
01/07/2000	New Zealand	Centre						Lost	5-71
7 matches			**2**	**1**	**0**	**0**	**12**		
Record			P: 7; W: 6; L: 1; Win%: 85.7						

South Africa U21 score first

SOUTH AFRICA U23

Date	Opponents	Position	T	C	P	D	Pts	Result	Score*
19/08/2000	SA Barbarians	Flyhalf	1	7	1		22	Won	62-34
29/11/2000	Netherlands	Flyhalf (R)						Won	100-10
02/12/2000	Portugal	Flyhalf						Won	36-15
07/12/2000	Tunisia	Flyhalf (R)						Won	47-15
14/12/2000	Morocco	Flyhalf (R)						Won	44-14
5 matches			**1**	**7**	**1**	**0**	**22**		
Record			P: 5; W: 5; Win%: 100						

South Africa U23 score first

SOUTH AFRICA 'A'

Date	Opponents	Position	T	C	P	D	Pts	Result	Score*
26/06/2002	Argentina	Flyhalf		3	2		12	Won	42-36
25/06/2003	Argentina	Flyhalf		1			2	Drew	30-30
2 matches			**0**	**4**	**2**	**0**	**14**		
Record			**P: 2; W: 1; D: 1; Win%: 50**						

*South Africa 'A' score first

BATH (ALL COMPETITIONS)

Date	Opponents	Position	T	C	P	D	Pts	Result	Score*
10/11/2007	Auch	Flyhalf	1				5	Won	28-6
17/11/2007	Parma	Flyhalf		1			2	Won	28-0
24/11/2007	Bristol	Flyhalf						Won	28-13
30/11/2007	Cardiff Blues	Flyhalf						Lost	6-14
07/12/2007	Albi	Flyhalf	1	2	4		21	Won	26-18
22/12/2007	Leeds	Flyhalf						Won	41-10
04/01/2008	Gloucester	Flyhalf						Won	10-5
12/01/2008	Parma	Flyhalf	1	1			7	Won	31-13
19/01/2008	Auch	Flyhalf			3		6	Won	31-13
27/01/2008	Saracens	Flyhalf	1				5	Lost	20-26
15/04/2008	Leicester	Flyhalf		1	3		11	Won	26-12
19/04/2008	Worcester	Flyhalf						Won	23-20
26/04/2008	Sale Sharks	Flyhalf						Won	36-14
03/05/2008	Saracens	Flyhalf	1				5	Won	66-21
10/05/2008	Gloucester	Flyhalf						Lost	6-8
18/05/2008	London Wasps	Flyhalf						Lost	10-21
25/05/2008	Worcester (F)	Flyhalf			1		3	Won	24-16
07/09/2008	Bristol	Flyhalf		3	4		18	Won	33-20
13/09/2008	Gloucester	Flyhalf						Lost	17-21
20/09/2008	London Irish	Flyhalf	1		2		11	Won	20-16
27/09/2008	Worcester	Flyhalf		3	2		12	Won	37-19
01/10/2008	London Wasps	Flyhalf		2	1		7	Won	27-23
12/10/2008	Toulouse	Flyhalf			2		6	Lost	16-18
19/10/2008	Newport	Flyhalf		1	2		8	Won	13-9
15/11/2008	Leicester	Flyhalf	1	2	2		15	Won	25-21
22/11/2008	Northampton	Flyhalf		2	3		13	Drew	28-28
30/11/2008	Harlequins	Flyhalf			3		9	Lost	14-21

BATH (ALL COMPETITIONS) *(continued)*									
Date	Opponents	Position	T	C	P	D	Pts	Result	Score*
07/12/2008	Glasgow	Flyhalf		3	3		15	Won	35-31
14/12/2008	Glasgow	Flyhalf		1	1		5	Won	25-19
20/12/2008	Sale Sharks	Flyhalf		1	4		14	Won	24-20
27/12/2008	Northampton	Flyhalf		2	2		10	Won	25-14
04/01/2009	Leicester	Flyhalf		2	1		7	Lost	22-24
18/01/2009	Newport	Flyhalf		1	1		5	Won	15-12
25/01/2009	Toulouse	Flyhalf			1		3	Drew	3-3
14/02/2009	Worcester	Flyhalf		4	2		14	Won	34-17
21/02/2009	London Irish	Flyhalf		1	1		5	Drew	20-20
28/02/2009	Gloucester	Flyhalf		3	2		12	Lost	27-36
07/03/2009	Bristol	Flyhalf		6	1		15	Won	45-8
15/03/2009	Saracens	Flyhalf		1	3		11	Lost	16-20
21/03/2009	Newcastle	Flyhalf		2	5		19	Won	36-25
01/04/2009	London Wasps	Flyhalf		1	5		17	Won	22-14
04/04/2009	Harlequins	Flyhalf			1		3	Lost	3-19
11/04/2009	Leicester	Flyhalf		1	1		5	Lost	15-20
19/04/2009	Newcastle	Flyhalf						Won	15-14
06/02/2010	Sale Sharks	Flyhalf						Won	40-7
14/02/2010	London Irish	Flyhalf						Won	35-22
20/02/2010	Worcester	Flyhalf						Won	37-13
27/03/2010	Harlequins	Flyhalf						Won	24-13
03/04/2010	Leicester	Flyhalf		1			2	Lost	20-43
17/04/2010	Sale Sharks	Flyhalf						Won	34-15
24/04/2010	London Wasps	Flyhalf						Won	35-19
08/05/2010	Leeds	Flyhalf						Won	39-3
16/05/2010	Leicester	Flyhalf						Lost	6-15
18/12/2010	Ulster	Flyhalf						Lost	22-26
01/01/2011	London Irish	Flyhalf						Won	25-24
08/01/2011	Leeds	Flyhalf						Won	16-13
15/01/2011	Aironi	Flyhalf						Won	55-16
22/01/2011	Biarritz	Flyhalf						Lost	19-26
11/02/2011	Sale Sharks	Flyhalf						Won	19-7
19/02/2011	Northampton	Flyhalf						Won	38-8
26/02/2011	Exeter Chiefs	Flyhalf						Won	12-9
05/03/2011	Gloucester	Flyhalf		1			2	Lost	22-34

BATH (ALL COMPETITIONS) *(continued)*									
Date	Opponents	Position	T	C	P	D	Pts	Result	Score*
26/03/2011	Leicester	Flyhalf			2		6	Lost	6-37
03/04/2011	Saracens	Flyhalf			3		9	Lost	9-20
09/04/2011	Exeter Chiefs	Flyhalf		1	3		11	Won	26-18
16/04/2011	Harlequins	Flyhalf		1	4		14	Won	19-15
30/04/2011	Newcastle	Flyhalf			2		6	Won	14-11
07/05/2011	Newcastle	Flyhalf		3	3		15	Won	42-12
68 matches			7	57	80	0	389		
Record		**P: 68; W: 46; L: 19; D: 3; Win%: 67.6**							

*Bath score first

INDEX

INDEX